LIGHT IN THE DARKNESS

Sammy Tippit

Sammy Tippit Books

Table of Contents

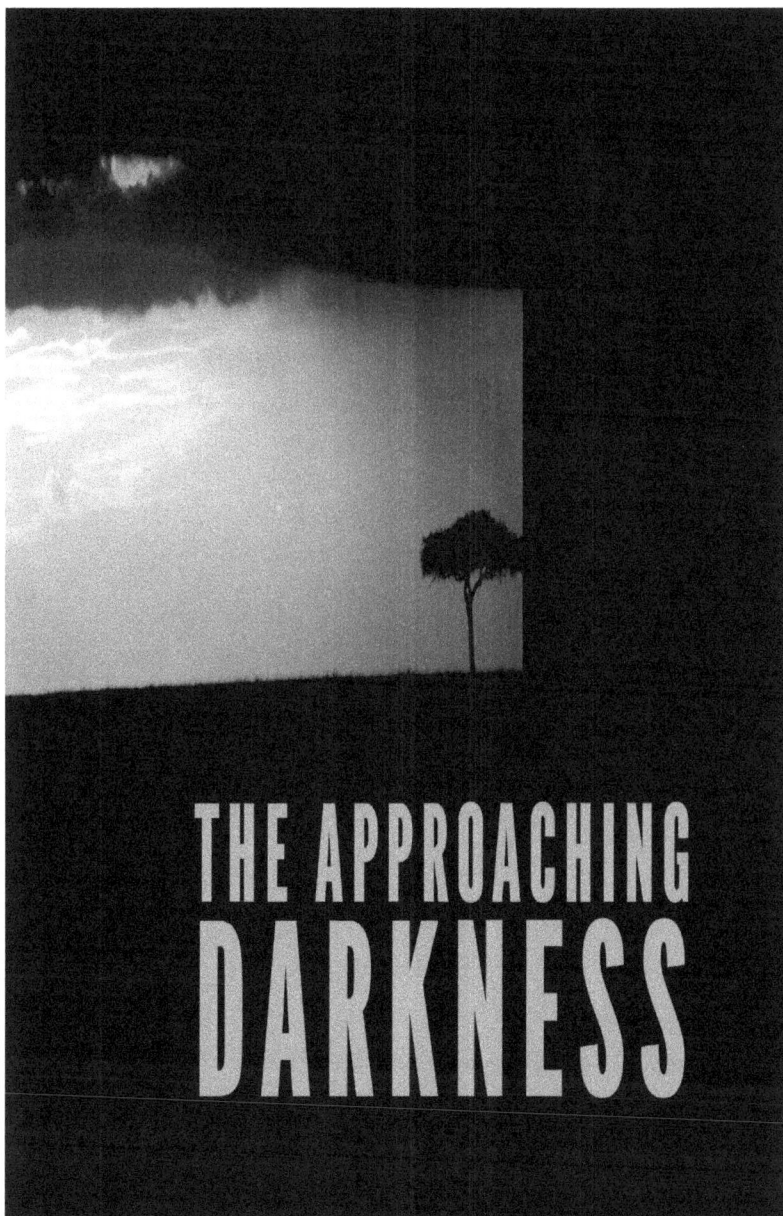

Chapter 1
The Approaching Darkness

A chill ran up my spine as I considered the possibility of going to a country where terrorists had decapitated an American journalist. The stakes couldn't have been higher. Seven of the men sitting around the table had counseled me when I had previously faced this kind of darkness, but it was the first time for the other five to give input about how to deal with this horrible evil.

I cleared my throat as I spoke to the Board of Directors of our ministry. "I'm willing to die for my faith, but I–" My lips trembled. "I don't want to go through what I've been reading about and seeing in the media." Sudden tears welled in my eyes. "I love my wife, and I want to spend many more years with her. I want to watch my grandchildren grow up." I didn't know what else to say. The silence that engulfed the room demanded that God's wisdom chair the remainder of the meeting.

My last visit to Pakistan had been nearly ten years prior to sharing those thoughts with the Board of Directors of our ministry. During that time, I had spoken about Jesus to large crowds in Faisalabad, Lahore, and Karachi, and many responded to the gospel. It was a wonderful season of encouraging Christians and explaining the love of God. Christian leaders were excited about the possibility of my return to the country.

After I left Pakistan, Christians translated and produced many of my messages in a digital format and distributed them throughout the nation. Christian leaders utilized the messages to teach in villages and communities surrounding the major cities. One Christian leader translated them into Pashto, a major language in Afghanistan, and many Afghans readily embraced the gospel.

A year later, my Pashto translator felt his life was in danger and asked us to hire a bodyguard. We agreed and made plans for a staff member to travel to Pakistan and provide technical assistance. We found a *safe house* for the work, but our staff member never made it to Pakistan.

A couple of weeks before he was scheduled to leave, I received a phone call that left me stunned. Terrorists had kidnapped my Pakistani colleague along with his bodyguard and demanded a large ransom. I didn't know how to respond and was left speechless. Before I could make a decision, I received another call. Our colleague and his bodyguard had been brutally murdered.

My stomach knotted. I was overwhelmed with a sense of grief and guilt – grief over the barbaric murder of a friend and colleague and guilt because he had likely been killed because of his work with our ministry. The terrorists had taken the laptop that held all my translated messages. Pakistani Pastors sent me an urgent but simple message: "You are on their radar. Don't return anytime soon. Wait until things settle down. We'll let you know when it's safe."

I waited – for seven years. Then, Pakistani Christian leaders contacted me, asking me to come back. They felt enough time had passed and that my ministry was needed. I agreed to go, but had a full travel schedule. After finding an agreeable date, we decided I would come during the first part of October, 2013.

Our Board of Directors was scheduled to meet on September 23, 2013, the week prior to my departure for Pakistan. The day before the Board meeting, two suicide bombers approached a crowd of Christians gathering for a luncheon and detonated their bombs, killing nearly 100 and wounding many more. It was one of the largest mass murders of Christians in the recent history of Pakistan.

The Board of Directors of our ministry was left with a major decision. The murder of my translator years earlier complicated any decision about my travel to Pakistan. It placed my name in the line of fire of radical Islamists. I've always relied on our friends and hosts in country to give me a sense of the danger as well as wisdom for conducting ministry in those dark and dangerous places. However, the two primary leaders in Pakistan weren't completely reassuring about the trip. One felt I should come. The other wasn't certain.

A third complication arose. Our ministry has a policy that I should never travel alone – especially to dark and difficult places. A colleague had applied for a visa, but the Pakistani Embassy didn't grant it. However, they gave one to me. That was surprising because we thought I might be denied a visa because of my visibility in the country, and my colleague would be given one because he wasn't doing any public ministry. The government's decision meant I would have to travel alone if we decided I should go.

After much prayer and a couple of Skype calls with Pakistani Christian leaders, we decided it was God's will that I travel to Pakistan for the pastors' conference and large outdoor evangelistic meetings. The pastor who thought we should continue with our plans felt this was a critical moment for Christians in the nation. Darkness had covered the land, and they needed the light of God's word to dispel the darkness. We decided to move the pastors' conference from a public place in the center of Karachi to the Marriott Hotel. The hotel had many layers of security and would make it a much safer venue for the pastors. It would also give us time to assess the situation and determine whether we should continue with the large public evangelistic meetings.

On October 6, 2013, I boarded a flight to Karachi, Pakistan. There was no travel companion, only the indwelling presence of Christ. I stared out the window as the flight rose above the clouds and wondered if I'd ever see my family again. I set my jaw and pulled back my shoulders. God gave me peace and direction through our Board. I took a deep breath as I stared out the window. *Oh, God, I trust You to lead every step of the way and every minute of the day.*

I was pleased when I arrived at the Marriott Hotel where I stayed for the entire time in Pakistan. There were multiple security barriers to get into the parking lot – then more security to reach the lobby. That produced a sense of confidence in my heart, but I knew my safety ultimately rested in God's hands. His presence flooded my heart the first evening. I thanked Him for safe travel and trusted Him to work in this needy situation.

A large ballroom was packed the next day with pastors and Christian leaders. The Spirit of God swept through the crowd. Hearts were renewed and spirits restored. Tears ran down the faces of the Pakistani Christian leaders. A spark of revival was ignited in hundreds of hungry hearts. I knew I had made the right decision. God had shattered the darkness enveloping the hearts of these Pakistani leaders. Fear turned into faith, and a sense of helplessness was transformed into a feeling of hopefulness. God visited His people.

The real test came during the evangelistic meetings that followed the pastors' conference. I didn't know if anyone would attend the public meetings because of terrorist threats against Christians throughout the country. Would people risk attending such a public forum in which the gospel of Jesus was proclaimed? Again, I was surprised. Thousands gathered on the grounds of the Church of Pakistan in the center of Karachi. I preached and many responded to the message, placing their faith in Jesus and making commitments to follow Him.

After returning to the Marriott from the first evangelistic meeting, I spent time in prayer – then called my wife, Tex, to let her know I was safe and give a report on all God had done. The adrenaline ran high, and it was difficult to sleep. I tried to make up for the lack of sleep with a strong cup of coffee on Friday morning, October 11. The aroma made me feel like I was back home in a local coffee shop. That feeling quickly dissipated when the waiter handed me a local English language newspaper. The headlines screamed across the top, "Bomb Blasts Rock the Four Provincial Capitals." The subheading continued, "10 killed, 60 injured, three suspected terrorists die." After reading the article, I asked the waiter if he had another English language paper. He brought me three others. The headlines were the same.

I swallowed hard and blew out a large breath of air. Terrorists had killed and maimed innocent people in every Provincial Capital, except one: Karachi, the city where we were conducting our evangelistic meetings. They had attempted to set off their bombs there, but the three suspected terrorists were killed when their bombs exploded on the way to their intended target. I slowly shook my head as I read the account. *Who was the intended target?*

No one had the answer to that question, but it was certain that our meeting would have been high on the list. The terrorists hated Americans and Christians. Our meeting definitely qualified as a target.

What transpired during the next few days went far beyond what I could have ever imagined. Thousands of Pakistanis heard the good news of God's love and responded to the message of the gospel. My heart was deeply touched by the large response of young men between the ages of 18 and 30. Many hundreds of them were the same age as those the terrorists recruited for the jihad. However, the Holy Spirit captured their hearts, and they placed their faith in Jesus and followed Him. The darkness attempted to keep the light out of the country, but the light shattered the darkness. God moved in a mighty way as the radiance of God's glory was seen in the nation.

When I returned to the United States, hope engulfed my heart. I knew the darkness could never extinguish the light dwelling inside the followers of Jesus. I had witnessed light in one of the most dangerous places on the planet and at one of the darkest moments. I met believers who continually faced persecution, and I learned much from these dear Christians.

ℰↄ

The Darkness Moves West

Nearly a year after my trip to Pakistan, I once again prepared to host our ministry Board meeting and report about the glorious light I had witnessed in Pakistan. As I prepared for the gathering, I watched in horror as reports of the beheading of an American journalist by Islamic terrorists filled the Internet and television. I listened intently to seasoned scholars, politicians, and military strategists talk about the threat of ISIS (Islamic State of Iraq and Syria) and Al Qaeda and the needed response of the Western world.

I respect every view and thought on the matter and believe that intense debate and actions are needed. I'm not a politician, or military expert, nor an expert on Islamic terrorism. However, I've become increasingly burdened that all of the discussion has missed one of the most important elements of the terrorist movement. It's a deeply spiritual crusade, which has wrapped itself in darkness for centuries.

There are certainly military, political, and ideological elements of the jihadists that must be addressed. However, if we don't come to grips with the spiritual dimension of this looming worldwide darkness, I'm concerned that our children and grandchildren in the Western world will face barbaric acts of persecution we never imagined possible. The children of many of my friends and colleagues in other countries already face such terror. Smart bombs, ideological debates, and political correctness can't shatter the darkness dwelling in the human heart. Only a display of the glory of God has the ability to expose and enlighten such hearts. We need a supernatural visitation from heaven – a revival much like the ones that our forefathers built as the foundation for Western civilization.

However, such a need exposes a great problem for the Western world. While the darkness of radical Islam grows, the church has been rocked to sleep in the bed of apathy. We've pulled the covers over our heads and said, "Night is approaching. We need our rest. All will be better in the morning." Others have gone the opposite direction and joined a choir that sings only one song: *political power and military might.*

However, we must never forget the bright and shining light that has been the foundation for Western civilization. It's that light which has guided us through the darkest nights and will lead us victoriously into the future. The United States was birthed in a mighty spiritual revival, which many historians have called the *First Great Awakening*. The *Second Great Awakening* followed at the beginning of the 1800s, and the *Great Prayer Revival* engulfed the major cities prior to the Civil War. A minor awakening occurred during the late 1960s and early 1970s during what the media dubbed as *The Jesus Movement*. Each one of those outpourings of God's Spirit came at very critical moments in American history.

This may be the most pivotal moment not only in the history of Western Civilization, but also the entire world. That may sound like an exaggeration of the situation. However, if you understand the goals of groups like ISIS and Al Qaeda, then you realize the barbarianism we've seen in Iraq, Syria, Nigeria, and Somalia could easily spread throughout the Middle East and quickly engulf the entire planet.

ℰꙮ

The Approaching Darkness

At the time of this writing, it's believed that thousands of jihadists with ISIS have come from Western Europe and hundreds from the United States and Canada. The great concern for Western law enforcement officials is that these terrorists carry Western passports, which enable them to move easily throughout Europe and North America. The United States and Britain have already seen savage murders on our streets and in our workplaces by those claiming to be jihadists.

If Christians understood the purpose and goals of these terrorist groups, we would be driven to our knees to cry to God for a mighty outpouring of His Spirit. ISIS terror leaders have claimed to establish a "caliphate" (khilafa in Arabic, which means succession) in Syria and Iraq. According to Wikipedia, a caliphate "is an Islamic state led by a supreme religious and political leader known as a *caliph* – i.e. 'successor' – to Muhammad. The succession of Muslim empires that have existed in the Muslim world are usually described as 'caliphates.' Conceptually, a caliphate represents a sovereign state of the entire Muslim faithful ruled by a caliph under Islamic law (*sharia*)."

Most people don't understand the historical significance of the Islamic caliphate. Mohammed's father-in-law was selected as a successor to Mohammed in 632 A.D. and was chosen as the first of many caliphs to follow. The Ottoman Empire stood as the last caliphate. It dissolved in 1924, a year after the birth of the Turkish Republic and shortly following the conclusion of World War I. Many historians see the beginning of the end of the last caliphate as September 11, 1683, when the Ottomans were defeated in the Battle of Vienna. Islam was rebuffed in a military struggle that kept Europe from possibly becoming an Islamic caliphate. One can only shudder to think what European history would have been had that battle been won by Islam.

This defeat continues to be a deep wound in the hearts of Muslim extremists. An objective observer cannot let the date of defeat go unnoticed – September 11. The ultimate goal of the caliphate was and is a world under the control of Islam, and one in which Sharia law is the way of life. Allan Hall, correspondent for AGE Media outlet in Australia, reported on a book written by Jordanian journalist Fouad Hussein. Hall wrote the following on August 24, 2005 in an online edition of AGE (http://www.

theage.com.au/news/war-on-terror/alqaeda-chiefs-reveal-world-domination-design/2005/08/23/1124562861654.html):

> *Al-Qaeda views its struggle as a long-term war with seven distinct phases.... Phase six, from 2016 on, will be a period of "total confrontation". As soon as the caliphate has been declared, the "Islamic army" will instigate the "fight between the believers and the non-believers" that has so often been predicted by al-Qaeda's leader, Osama bin Laden.*
>
> *Phase seven, the final stage, is described as "definitive victory".*

Hussein writes that, in the terrorists' eyes, the caliphate will succeed because 1.5 billion Muslims will have destroyed the resolve of the rest of the world. They believe this phase will be completed by 2020.

഻

The Christian Response

Many Christians find themselves confused about the needed response. Most seem content to sleep during this dark hour. The premise of this book and the larger series is that spiritual darkness lies at the core of the situation we face today, and followers of Jesus possess the light that can shatter the darkness. We have dwelling within us the hope of the glory of God.

This book and the series are filled with truths learned from believers who live in some of the darkest places on the planet. It's filled with stories that originated from countries like Iran, Pakistan, and Somalia – the hiding places of many terrorists.

It's written from seeing the glory of God in the aftermath of the genocide in Rwanda. It comes from having carried the light of the gospel into war zones such as Burundi, Democratic Republic of Congo, and Liberia. It grows out of decades of ministry in communist countries during the dark days in Eastern Europe. You'll read the stories of unknown believers who have proven to be spiritual giants in their homelands.

The Christian community in North America and Western Europe must rally in prayer for a great outpouring of God's Spirit at this critical moment in history. At the close of some chapters, you will find links to websites, which contain devotional and practical information about spiritual awakening in America. I encourage you to visit these organizations and ministries frequently and immerse yourself in the history and truths about revival.

As we see the darkness swiftly approaching, I offer this work as a clarion call for Christians to do as the Scriptures say and put on the "whole armor of God" and let their "light shine." A battle is raging for the hearts of women and men around the world. We face those who march to the drumbeat of hate. However, hate surrenders to those who carry weapons loaded with love. Our weapons are not filled with bombs that wreak death and destruction. When we use the weapons given us, love spreads so rapidly that it brings life to all in its path and transforms the course of history. Darkness is dispersed, and the light of God's glory rises. Heaven visits earth. Revival descends. The world is changed. Hate can never defeat love when that love is exercised in the power of the One whose nature is love. The light of God's love will dispel the darkness.

❧

Websites with Resources for Spiritual Awakening

Campus Renewal Ministries: https://www.campusrenewal.org

Harvest Prayer Ministries: http://www.harvestprayer.com/
resources/articles

Heart Cry for Revival: http://heart-cryforrevival.org

Herald of His Coming: http://www.heraldofhiscoming.com

Life Action Ministries: https://www.lifeaction.org

Revive Our Hearts: https://www.reviveourhearts.com

Sammy Tippit Books: http://www.sammytippitbooks.com

Sammy Tippit Ministries: http://sammytippit.org

Refresh Conference: http://refreshconference.org

Bomb blasts rock the four provincial capitals

10 killed, over 60 injured; three suspected terrorists die

By our correspondents

KARACHI/LAHORE/PE-SHAWAR/QUETTA: Thursday proved to be another tragic day for the country as the four provincial capitals were rocked with bomb blasts killing as many as 10 people and injuring over 60.

The worst incident took place in Quetta where a powerful bomb, apparently aimed at targeting the police, ripped through the main shopping area, killing six people and wounding 42 others.

The bomb exploded outside the City Police Station in Liaquat

Continued on page 4
Related story, picture on page 13

LAHORE: Rescue workers busy in their work following a blast in the Old Anarkali area here on Thursday. —— APP photo

Chapter 2
Prayer in the Darkness

ISIS and Al Qaeda aren't the only forms of darkness facing Christians at this critical moment in history. Global darkness has the ability to penetrate the shores of every country via the Internet and through the ease of international transportation. A terrorist leader made use of the Internet in September, 2014 and gave a command to his followers. Not long afterwards an extremist decapitated one of his co-workers in the heartland of the United States. With today's technology, it seems almost inevitable that the world will quickly be inundated with such tales of terror.

However, there's not only a growing global darkness, but also a deepening domestic darkness. It doesn't just dwell in a far away desert in the Middle East, but it can easily be seen spreading throughout Western culture like a seismic tidal wave. I'm convinced that the epicenter of this darkness lies within the family. The collapse of the family unit has left a moral and spiritual vacuum. We don't have to go very far to be sucked into its dark hole. It can be found on any street where the spiritual power source has been disrupted, leaving many homes without any guiding light. Anger, abuse, and base behavior have run rampant down Main Street and now threaten to engulf entire communities.

Perhaps the greatest darkness facing each of us is the inner darkness dwelling in the human heart. Most of us would like to say, "The global darkness is really bad, and the darkness down the street is shocking." However, few are willing to ask God to search our own hearts and expose the dark areas of our own lives. Each of us has hidden corners in our hearts we've kept under lock and key. We've closed off these areas to the searchlight of the Holy Spirit. David, a leader who was described as "a man after God's own heart" once said, "Search me, O God, and know my heart! Try me and know my thoughts! And see if there be any grievous way in me, and lead me in the way everlasting!" (Psalm 139:23 ESV).

✍

The Power of Authentic Prayer

It's this kind of deeply intimate prayer that carries the power to expose and expel the darkness. This isn't the first moment in which history has displayed such deep darkness. There's an entire era described as the *Dark Ages*. Yet, God's brightest light has always shone at the darkest moments. Historians often refer to these times as *Great Awakenings*.

Mighty prayer movements have preceded every great historical and Biblical revival. Spiritual awakening always descends on the wings of a handful of praying men and women. As darkness covers a community, someone comes under a great burden to pray and seek God's face. The Holy Spirit responds to such cries and enlightens hearts, communities, and even entire nations. As people carrying light fill the community, the darkness is dispelled.

Revival comes. Communities are awakened and lives transformed. God moves in mighty power.

ℰℛ

The Power of Prayer in Iran

There's no place too dark for God's light to penetrate and no heart too difficult to be set aflame by His love. I was the keynote speaker at a conference in Northern California in 1998. I spoke each evening while others spoke during the day sessions. One of the speakers made a shocking statement in his session. "I understand that Sammy Tippit goes to the difficult and dangerous areas of the world. Our organization has determined that the most dangerous country in the world at this moment is Iran. I challenge Sammy Tippit to go to Iran and pray for God to open the door for the gospel."

I gasped. I wasn't sure how to respond as I listened to the speaker call me out. Crawl under the seat and hide, or sit and smile. I decided upon the latter, but after his speech, I introduced myself and invited him to join me for lunch. God spoke deeply to my heart during that meeting. I listened to the gentleman share his deep burden for one of the darkest places on Earth. He talked about Christians who had been imprisoned for their faith. Goosebumps rose on my arms as he described the martyrdom of some of the Christian leaders in Iran. He asked me to go there and pray for an open door for the gospel. I was overwhelmed by his compassion and sensed God's Spirit leading me to give a positive answer to his challenge.

I cleared my throat and was about to respond when he said, "There's one thing I haven't told you yet." I immediately tilted my head and shot him a quizzical look. He flashed a broad grin.

"Americans aren't allowed into Iran at this time. You'll have to pray for God to allow you in the country before you can go there and pray for God to open doors for the gospel."

I could only shake my head. "You've got to be kidding."

He wasn't. He and I spent several months praying for doors to open in Iran. Then I received a call from my friend. "The government of Iran is giving visas to Americans. Do you want to go?"

I was ready. Ten of us quietly met in a hotel in Europe prior to catching our flight into Iran. There were no big name Christian personalities – only a few people with hearts to seek God on behalf of the nation of Iran. We made a covenant not to speak to anyone about Christ. As an evangelist, I knew it would take a great amount of personal discipline. Our mission was simple – pray!

We spent ten days walking the streets of Tehran, Isfahan, Shiraz, and other cities. We prayed as we walked. To the casual observer, we were tourists, but something significant was transpiring in our hearts. We were communing with the Creator of the universe, crying to Him for an outpouring of His Spirit upon the nation.

I was caught by surprise by several things. I was amazed by the love that most Iranians had for Americans. I had only seen the opposite on television: people filled with hate chanting, "Death to America!" There were certainly radical Islamists who hated Americans, but most of the people we encountered were thrilled when they learned we came from the United States. They loved us.

I was astonished by a second observation. Scores of satellite dishes dotted the rooftops of the apartment buildings and houses. Most were illegal. However, people desperately wanted information from the outside world. As I walked the streets of Isfahan one day, God's Spirit tugged at my heartstrings. I stopped and stared at the satellite dishes and heard a small still voice. "That's how you will bring the gospel to the Iranian people." I felt my blood rushing as I sensed God's heart for the Iranian people.

When I returned to the United States, I joined my colleague in southern California where more than one million Iranians live. We met with Iranian Christian leaders and discussed how we might be able to help Iranian Christians. They suggested several ways in which we could contribute to God's work in the U.S. One pastor quickly rattled a list of needs. "First, we need your books in Farsi (the Persian language). We need your website translated into Farsi. You need to train our leaders."

I was overwhelmed with their ideas, and my thoughts ran in every direction. I told them I was ready to help, but had no idea how to complete any of the tasks they mentioned. That meeting began a relationship with the Iranian Christian community that has lasted for many years. It thrust me into a ministry among Iranians, and I've been amazed at the work of God. Perhaps, the greatest movement of God's Spirit in Islamic nations has been taking place among Iranians themselves. Thousands of them have had dreams and visions of Jesus and followed Him.

I've listened to many of their stories, and most have the same storyline but a different set of circumstances. It goes something like this. "I had a problem. (Some went through sickness, others divorce, and some had attempted suicide.) I cried to Allah and he did not answer me. I felt hopeless. I then had a dream. (Some had visions.) I saw Jesus. I asked people to explain the dream. A Christian told me about Jesus, and I believed in Him as the Son of God."

All included the same basic experience of having encountered Jesus in a dream or vision. I often asked how they knew it was Jesus and they told me, "By the nail prints in His hands and feet."

After a couple of years of ministry with Iranians, my colleague told me, "God has opened a door for a television broadcast via satellite into Iran. Are you willing?"

I was more than willing. I immediately found a lonely place on a nearby beach where I took a moment to worship God. Tears ran down my cheeks. "You're so wonderful! You are faithful to keep your promises. I love You! I love You!"

God worked in many more significant ways, some of which I'm not able to mention publicly. However, there was one thing that occurred that confounds me to this day. I was doing some research in North Carolina for a book when I received an email from a friend who lives in Iran. "Sammy, you're not going to believe this, but your story of your faith in Jesus is on the homepage of one of the most prestigious universities in the country."

I felt like Abraham when God told him he would have a child in his old age. The Bible says, "Then Abraham fell on his face and laughed and said to himself, 'Shall a child be born to a man who is a hundred years old? Shall Sarah, who is ninety years old, bear a child?'" (Genesis 17:17 ESV). It seemed ludicrous to Abraham that he and Sarah could have a child when they were at the century mark in life. His first response was, "This has to be a joke."

At that moment, I understood Abraham's lack of faith because I wanted to laugh at what had been told me. It couldn't be true that a prestigious university in the center of one of the world's darkest nations would put my Christian story on their home page. I immediately sent emails to other Iranian friends. "Could this be true? If so, have they changed my story in any way?"

The response sent chills up my spine. "It's not only true, but they have quoted it exactly as you have it on your website. They even keep the part where you invite people to pray and give their hearts to Jesus."

I found a private place of prayer. My throat was so tight it was difficult to speak. I sat for several minutes in stillness and was reminded of the promise in Psalms, "Be still, and know that I am God. I will be exalted among the nations; I will be exalted in the earth!" (Psalms 46:10 ESV).

I learned that there's no place too difficult for God. Nothing is impossible with Him. He specializes in shattering the darkness. He could and will destroy the darkness in one millisecond. However, He's chosen to work through people; humble, holy, praying people. He's looking for people who will seek Him. It doesn't matter whether the darkness is down the street, in another country, or deep within our own hearts. His light dispels the darkness.

℃℈

Prayer that Dispels Darkness

Prayer is universal and some form of it can be found in all cultures. Devout Muslims pray five times per day. Hindus, Buddhists, Jews, and Christians have different forms of praying. However, the kind of prayer I'm talking about is not a "form of prayer." It's not religious praying, but intimate communion.

Prayer is not a religious duty, but rather a Divine encounter. It's not an attempt to reach up to God, but it's walking by faith into His holy presence. It's not a work for God, but a resting place in His grace. It's not doing something for God, but accepting what Jesus did for us. It's only because of the cross that we have access into His presence. It is joy unspeakable – intimacy with the Creator. We love Him because He loved us first. We have access into His presence because the Lamb of God has forgiven us.

Many Christians don't pray because they think it's a religious duty and don't realize it's a grace relationship. Prayer is laborious for many, but it's delightful for those who understand that we have been granted access into the presence of the One who is absolute purity. Because Jesus provided us forgiveness when He died on the cross, we are able to enter into a deep and intimate relationship with a holy God. Once I understood that truth, everything changed. Prayer ceased to be dreaded drudgery and became divine delight.

When we understand that we come into His presence by grace, it produces praise for who He is and thanksgiving for all He's done. It ushers us into true worship. When prayer is rooted in His perfect love rather than our human obligation, it sets us free from fear. We don't fear His light searching our hearts. We know that His desires are always good. We allow His light to shine in any area of our lives because we know His goodness always produces what is best for us. Even though we know that the darkness of our hearts will be exposed, we realize His plan is perfect. It's this kind of intimate prayer that ushers in the dawn of a new era.

☙

Elements of Prayer that Shatter the Darkness

As I've walked into the dark areas of the world, I've seen several common elements of prayer that dispel darkness. The first: transparency. The darkness often drives God's people to find a place of safety, and His presence is the most secure spot on this planet. Because of His perfect love, all fear is cast out. Because He is full of grace, we can be completely honest. There's no need to allow guilt or deception to dwell in our hearts because the way into His presence is through the cross. By His death, we are made clean. No need for fear. No place for guilt. Honesty and change flood our souls as the light casts out darkness.

When we allow His light to shine into the secret places of our hearts, we're already on the road to revival. It produces deep confession and complete repentance. Confession brings freedom from the darkness and repentance produces great peace and joy. The change in our lives is the light, which leads us to a highway called holiness. That highway leaves no room for pride. We are escorted onto the highway by the Holy Spirit and can only continue the journey by His amazing grace. We travel the road leading to revival because God's grace is manifested in our lives.

The second characteristic of prayer that shatters the darkness is a deep sense of desperation. I shared the platform with the Distinguished Professor of Evangelism at Southwestern Baptist Theological Seminary, Dr. Roy Fish, several months before he passed. During a question and answer session, a pastor asked him, "Do you see any hope for revival in America?"

His response was quite interesting. Dr. Fish replied, "The great hope I see is that there is a growing feeling of hopelessness in the Christian community."

Historically, revival has swept the Christian community when believers became hopeless. Once they realized that their methods and material resources couldn't chase out the darkness, they cried in desperation to God. Their hopelessness drove them to the only hope for humanity – Jesus. Look at the great moments of Biblical history and discover the desperation that precedes the radiance of God's glory.

Life looked hopeless for the children of Israel before Moses encountered God at the burning bush. The light radiating from that bush would usher God's glory into the lives of millions of Hebrews. Their future and freedom arose from the light displayed in an old bush in a desolate desert. We see a similar sense of hopelessness in the New Testament. The disciples were dispersed with a feeling of defeat when Jesus died on the cross. But the greatest manifestation of God's glory was just around the corner. He conquered death, hell, and the devil. The world has never been the same and that light continues to shine to this very day.

Desperation precedes divine visitation. Hopelessness drives us to a place upon which we hear the words, "Take your shoes off, for you are standing on holy ground." Doubt and fear lead us to the One who says, "I will be with you always." It's in such a place that desperate hearts are revived.

There's one more characteristic I've seen among those who have sought God in the darkness and became witnesses of the marvels of His light. There's been a passionate plea for the freedom of those trapped in the darkness. The most amazing thing transpires as God's people flee the darkness and run into His presence. Those who have been abused by the brokers of darkness pray with passion for their persecutors. They love those who hate them and pray for those who abuse them.

I ministered in Romania during the dark period of the evil communist dictator, Nicolae Ceaucescu. Christians had been severely persecuted under his rule. During that period, some friends and I took a Romanian friend out to eat in Bucharest. It was a nice restaurant on the top of a tall building. We were able to see much of the city. I was reminded of a passage from the Bible where Jesus lamented over Jerusalem. I began quoting the passage, but changing it to say, "O Bucharest, Bucharest, the city that kills the prophets and stones those who are sent to it! How often would I have gathered your children together as a hen gathers her brood under her wings..." (Matthew 23:37 ESV).

I wasn't able to complete quoting the verse. I glanced at my friend as he sat silently, weeping. I knew I was with a man who loved his people. We all sat in silence and wept. God's love poured over our souls in wave after wave.

An amazing miracle rises when we pray for revival. When we enter into intimate communion with God, He converts hate into love, anger into peace, and fear into courage. Passionate prayer transforms us into compassionate people. The love of God always produces a love for people and an abiding faith in His promises. It's in the place of faith that the darkness is dispelled.

∾

Websites with Resources on Prayer for Revival
http://www.onecry.com
http://sammytippit.org/devotions/a-sacred-connection/
http://www.harvestprayer.com
http://www.heartcrysa.com/prayer.html

Chapter 3
Faith in the Darkness

More than 500 years ago, a young man was riding horseback in a rural area of Germany when lightning struck nearby. After narrowly escaping, the young German feared death and was afraid of God's judgment. Not long after he entered a monastery in Erfurt where he studied the Scriptures. His life was transformed as he contemplated the Bible's statement, "The just shall live by faith." Those words rose in his heart like rays of light at dawn. They didn't just transform him, but changed the course of history in Europe. The words, "the just shall live by faith," echoed throughout the continent, and a reformation was birthed more than 100 years before the Islamic caliphate attempted to capture Europe.

Martin Luther wasn't the only reformer who allowed the light to shine at such a dark moment of history. John Calvin was awakened by the truth of Scriptures not long after Luther proclaimed God's word. While Luther preached in Germany, Calvin proclaimed God's word in Switzerland. A Latin phrase captured the hearts of the Reformers and the motto was inscribed on the words of their coins: *Post pennebras, lux,* which means *After darkness, light.*

The passionate words of the Reformers weren't merely platitudes rooted in the power of positive thinking. Light had burst into their hearts through the Scriptures, and deep convictions formed, leaving no room for darkness. Western civilization was enlightened. Although the Reformers were men and women with weaknesses like any other mortals, they understood that survival demanded faith in the midst of darkness.

This understanding of the necessity of faith wasn't unique to the Reformers. It's been the underpinning of Judaism and Christianity for thousands of years. The author of the book of Hebrews wrote under the inspiration of the Holy Spirit, "And without faith it is impossible to please Him, for whoever would draw near to God must believe that He exists and that He rewards those who seek Him" (Hebrews 11:6 ESV).

If you study the lives of those mentioned in that chapter, every great work accomplished was rooted in faith during very dark times. Before the flood, Noah built an ark by faith. Abraham birthed a nation by faith. Moses led the children of Israel out of slavery by faith. Joshua brought them into the land they had been promised by faith. David slew a giant by faith.

In the previous chapter we learned of the power of prayer. However, powerful praying must be accompanied by faith. Jesus said, "For truly, I say to you, if you have faith like a grain of mustard seed, you will say to this mountain, 'Move from here to there,' and it will move, and nothing will be impossible for you" (Matthew 17:20 ESV). Jesus explained that prayer plus faith had the ability to toss mountains into the sea. It doesn't matter how huge the mountains in our lives and communities seem to be, they are nothing for the woman or man of faith. It doesn't take a great scholar, successful businessperson, or powerful athlete to conquer the mountain. It only takes a humble, holy, praying person who exercises faith. It doesn't even take a person with a huge amount of faith, only one with faith like a grain of mustard seed.

I've been amazed at the childlike faith of some of the people God has used in the darkest places. These heroes are mostly unknown to the West but well known to God. Emmanuel Gyamfi, a Liberian pastor, has been on the front lines of the battle with the Ebola virus. His faith has not only amazed me, but has produced incredible assistance to a nation devastated by multiple waves of darkness.

I first had contact with Pastor Gyamfi in 2003. He had just started a church outside Monrovia, Liberia's capital. It grew rapidly as they saw people's lives changed. A war had been raging for more than a decade, and the situation seemed hopeless. Pastor Gyamfi prayed and asked God for guidance. He felt the only hope for the nation was a change in the heart of its citizens. He went online to see if he could find an evangelist to come to the nation and preach the gospel. He believed the gospel held the only hope to drive out the darkness.

He found hundreds of evangelistic ministries on the Internet. He prayed and asked God for wisdom. He then narrowed his search to eleven evangelists and wrote them, asking if they would come to Liberia and preach the gospel. I was the only one who answered his inquiry, and my response wasn't necessarily positive. I simply responded, asking, "Who are you? Give me more information on your background."

Pastor Gyamfi took my reply as God's leadership and stepped out in faith. He called my office – not once, but many times each week. I didn't want to speak with him until I knew more about him. However, he persisted, and I finally talked with him.

"Please come to Liberia. Our people are in great need. They are hungry for hope, for good news. I believe the Lord will bless our nation if you come and preach the gospel." Pastor Gyamfi's simple childlike faith touched me deeply.

He asked me to seek God about ministering in Liberia. I agreed, and God spoke to my heart. One of my staff, Chris Dillashaw, was scheduled to travel to Ghana to work with believers on an evangelism project. I invited Pastor Gyamfi to meet Chris in Accra, and I told Chris to spend time with the Liberian pastor to discern if he was authentic and his burden to reach his people was genuine. I knew that there were many scams birthed on the Internet, and I wanted to make sure he could be trusted.

Chris came back with a very positive report about Pastor Gyamfi, and I made plans to travel to Liberia. It wasn't easy for Pastor Gyamfi. The Liberian pastor described to Chris what took place. "Right before we were scheduled to meet, the rebels began to attack near the capital city and the airport area. God protected me, and saved my life."

When Pastor Gyamfi attempted to return home, the airport in Liberia was closed. He had to wait in Ghana for one month before he could return to his family. His church members feared the rebels as soldiers entered the area. A number of Pastor Gyamfi's flock fled to his home. When the pastor spoke by phone to his wife, she told him that forty-eight church members were living in their home!

During the conversation with his wife Ruth, she heard a loud banging on the door. The rebels were there. She quickly turned off the phone and hid it. Meanwhile, Pastor Gyamfi paced his room in Ghana and prayed. Tears flowed freely. Jesus was the only hope for his family and church members. It was a very dark moment, but he reached deep into his soul and trusted God to shine His light in his home in Liberia.

The rebels robbed his family of all their possessions but didn't kill anyone. Pastor Gyamfi bowed in worship when he heard the news. Once he returned home, we discussed a date for my coming to the war-torn nation. I traveled to the Lower Virginia community of Liberia in 2004. The war had just concluded. People received the message of Christ with great enthusiasm. They had finally come out of a very dark period, but were completely unaware of an even deeper darkness awaiting them.

God blessed the meetings wonderfully, and I returned to Liberia in 2007 and 2009. When I returned in 2007, I smiled when Pastor Gyamfi brought me to his church facility. While God had changed hearts, Pastor Gyamfi knew the people also needed medical treatment. The community was about a forty-five minute drive from medical facilities in Monrovia, and people in the community often needed immediate treatment. Most of them didn't have any means of transportation. People were dying, and Pastor Gyamfi's heart broke. He remembered how God had answered his prayer and sent someone to minister to the hearts of his people. This time, he prayed and asked God for help to minister to the health needs of his people. He did what he knew best to do. Pray, and go to the Internet!

A hospital in the United States responded and helped him construct a small clinic. After giving me a tour of the facility, he shared his burden. "We have a facility. We have nurses and doctors. But we don't have enough medicine. People are dying from malaria and stomach illnesses. Do you know a family in America who might help and provide medicines for us?"

My lips trembled. "Yeah, I think I know a family."

When my wife and I returned to the hotel, she asked, "Who is the family?"

I smiled. "We are."

When we returned to the United States, I approached my son and daughter and their spouses. "Would you like to join us in sponsoring medicine for this little clinic in Liberia?" They were all in. For the next couple of years, we helped provide medicine for the clinic, not realizing that it would become a light on a hill in a very dark place. I was deeply impressed with how Pastor Gyamfi gave such a thorough account for the money we provided. He gave detailed reports of how the medicine was dispersed as well as pictures and stories of patients who had been saved because of the medicine.

I shared with our ministry Board of Directors how God was using the small clinic to save lives. A deep concern grew in one of the board members, Dr. Brent Saathoff, and my son, Dave, to help the community. They started an organization, *Liberia Now*. They established a holistic approach to ministering to the community: providing clean water and sanitation, assisting young people with education, providing micro-loans, and training Christian leaders. A partnership was birthed with Pastor Gyamfi and his Liberian church.

The partnership produced a solid ministry during the next few years. During July and August of 2014, Dave and his family met Brent and a team from his church in Liberia. Brent was training leaders while Dave and his wife, Kelly, and their three children worked with the children in the community. However, a deep darkness crept across the border while they were there. Word spread that a dreaded and deadly disease, Ebola, was taking the lives of scores of Liberians.

People responded with fear and confusion. The government placed a ban on all public gatherings. The rapidly spreading darkness drove me to pray with a great sense of urgency for my son, daughter-in-law, grandchildren, colleagues, and Liberian friends.

Flights out of the country were being cancelled. My family and U.S. colleagues were able to leave the country without contracting the virus, but our Liberian friends were left to face a darkness that produced fear in hearts around the world.

I prayed for Pastor Gyamfi and his coworkers. I wondered what would happen to the clinic because the people most vulnerable to the virus were health care workers. Most clinics and hospitals closed down. But, my dear pastor friend and his team felt they couldn't close the clinic. Many more people were dying of other maladies than Ebola. He prayed and exercised faith and compassion. They kept the clinic open. They asked *Liberia Now* to provide proper protective gear for the clinic staff, which it did. It became one of the few clinics to remain open to assist the Liberian people during the darkness. Countless lives have been saved because of the faith of this courageous pastor. He refused to look at the darkness, but rather trusted God for his people.

While fear has been the greatest friend of Ebola, faith has been the greatest weapon of Christians. Fear and faith are foes. Fear points us inward, while faith points us upward. Fear paralyzes, while faith mobilizes. Fear makes us tremble, while faith moves our mountains. Fear grows in dark places, while faith emerges from humble hearts. Fear stalks in the shadows, while faith walks in the light.

As the darkness envelopes this generation, we need men and women who walk by faith, live by faith, and minister by faith. Such people will cast dark mountains into the sea. We must then ask, "What is faith and how do we obtain it?"

છ

Faith and Trust

Faith has a twin brother, but they're not identical. These two siblings have been birthed into the same family and have the same spiritual DNA, but they are also somewhat different. *Faith* and *trust* are both birthed by the character of God. As we come to know God, we are overwhelmed by His nature. We see His faithfulness to fulfill His promises. We experience His love in the midst of sorrow. We know His grace when we are broken. We bask in His goodness when we awaken each morning. We look at history and see His hand. We look at our lives and we see His heart. Trust grows in the soil of intimacy with Jesus. We trust Him because we have come to know Him as the One who is completely trustworthy. We trust Him in the darkness because He fills our souls with the light of His love, grace, goodness, and purity. Trust resides in the residence of confidence and assurance. It's the same dwelling of faith – a place of rest.

The Bible says, "Trust in the Lord with all your heart and do not lean on your own understanding. In all your ways acknowledge Him, and He will make straight your paths" (Proverbs 3:5, 6 ESV). Trust abides in a heart full of assurance because its focus is on God, not circumstances. It's able to rest because its confidence is firmly rooted in His character.

Faith and trust contain the same sense of confidence and assurance because they are birthed from the same Father. The Bible gives a clear definition of faith: "Now faith is the assurance of things hoped for, the conviction of things not seen" (Hebrews 11:1 ESV). Faith dwells in the same place of rest where trust lives. However, if we continue reading the chapter in Hebrews, we discover an additional feature of faith's DNA. Faith must be exercised in order for it to be faith. Faith takes the assurance birthed in our hearts because of God's character and puts trust into practice. The confidence we gain by trusting God enables us to take a step of faith. The added dimension that faith brings in our relationship with God produces works that please God and help others.

That's why each of the men and women of faith in Hebrews chapter eleven were called to some action. The action didn't save them. Their faith response saved them. However, it would not have been faith without their action. The Bible explains this truth in the book of James when it says, "Show me your faith apart from your works, and I will show you my faith by my works" (James 2:18 ESV). The author illustrates the truth with the example of Abraham. He states, "Was not Abraham our father justified by works when he offered up his son Isaac on the altar? You see that faith was active along with his works, and faith was completed by his works; and the promise of the Scripture was fulfilled that says, 'Abraham believed God, and it was counted to him as righteousness' - and he was called a friend of God" (James 2:21 – 23 ESV).

Faith produces works full of light because its focus is on the God who is light. Such works are rooted in a deep assurance and great confidence in the character of God. Faith without works is dead, and works without faith is like a man who swings at his enemy in the darkness but never knows the location of his foe. Faith works because it has emerged from the light, which gives great assurance and confidence. Faith rests in the character of God, and it works with the knowledge that the task is ultimately in God's hands.

Faith doesn't fear the mountain of darkness surrounding the human heart. It casts it into the sea. As darkness creeps into Western civilization, we once again need those who have the confidence to act upon the words of the Reformers, "*Post pennebras, lux* – After darkness, light." Pray! Trust God! Live and work as though the dawn is at hand!

To read the complete story of Pastor Emmanuel Gyamfi, visit the Liberia Now website: http://liberianow.org/category/loving-liberia/

Scroll down to article: Emmanuel Gyamfi Profile – *From Ruin to Restoration*

Chapter 4
Courage in the Darkness

Courage has been a primary characteristic of God's people during historical and Biblical revivals. Daniel dared to face a den of lions. Moses refused to be intimidated by Pharoah's threats. Gideon heard God's call and fought with a small band of men. The Holy Spirit transformed Peter from a spineless fisherman to a valiant preacher. When the early church was threatened, they prayed – then boldly proclaimed the gospel.

Darkness builds terror in our hearts, but God's love tears down every bit of fear that has been constructed. It's at the moment we feel the weakest that God's grace proves the strongest. His grace turns our timidity into gallantry and our fear into faith.

Darkness produces fear because of the unknown and unseen. Fear then rises in hearts because of what we can't see and don't understand. On the other hand, courage rises when faith dwells in our hearts. The Bible says, "Faith is the assurance of things hoped for, the conviction of things not seen" (Hebrews 11:1 ESV). Even though we can't see, our hearts develop a deep sense of assurance when we live by faith. Although there may be no evidence for our need, faith carves a place of conviction deep within our souls.

Many people struggle to become courageous. Prayer is the starting line for courage. When prayer is properly understood, it produces intimacy with God. The close communion with Him causes us to love and trust Him. Prayer bears the fruit of faith. When we rest in the confidence of His love, faith creates courage in our hearts. Fear can't control the courageous heart. When God fills men and women with courage, they become unstoppable on the eve of even the darkest nights.

I'll never forget the courageous men and women I met when I was asked to conduct a large Christian outreach in Egypt at the turn of the century. I preached in a central location, and Christians gathered in more than 600 church facilities throughout the nation and listened via video. It was estimated that more than 120,000 people watched the broadcast nightly. I was overwhelmed by God's blessings.

We also conducted a conference for pastors who came from multiple nations in the Middle East. I met some of the most wonderful Christian leaders I've ever known. A couple of men from Sudan talked with me about coming to their country for similar meetings. They were extremely humble and unflinching in their faith. Christians in Sudan had scheduled a large celebratory service in Khartoum during the previous Easter season. They invited a well-known Christian from Germany to speak. However, government authorities threatened the Christians and refused to allow the meetings.

Christians from many denominations gathered early that Sunday morning in the Anglican Church in Khartoum to celebrate the death, burial, and resurrection of Jesus. Soldiers arrived at the worship service and fired on the crowd. Bullets pierced believers, leaving blood splattered on church walls. One of the leaders fixed his eyes on me. "We want you to come to Khartoum in September and preach in the stadium."

I shifted beneath his gaze. "But would they allow…?

"God will make a way. But, we must never surrender to fear."

I rubbed the back of my neck. "I'll pray about it. But there is one thing that must be certain. It's imperative that we have government permission."

My Sudanese friend smiled. "That is impossible, but God will show us His favor. He will make a way."

I gave myself to prayer and sensed it was God's will to join my Christian friends in Khartoum. After much correspondence, we decided upon a date to minister in the Republic of Sudan. I would travel to Khartoum in October 2001 to conduct a large outreach event. We took a huge step of faith and trusted God to give us favor with the government. We knew it would take a miracle. President Bill Clinton had previously bombed a pharmaceutical factory in Khartoum because the United States had intelligence that indicated it was a cover for a chemical weapons plant. Osama bin Laden had lived in Khartoum before moving to Afghanistan. Al Qaeda was still operating in Khartoum. From a human perspective, the darkness made our goals unattainable. However, these courageous believers refused to yield to fear.

Christians set up an organizational structure to enable them to secure the necessary permission from government leaders to conduct the meetings. Their work proved successful, and leaders called me in June, 2001. They were so excited as they shared the good news with me that I had to ask them to slow their speech. "We have received verbal agreement from the government to allow the meetings. You will be able to preach in the stadium!"

I tried to sound positive, but secretly doubt ran rampant in my heart. "Um," I cleared my throat. "Have the authorities put the permission in writing?"

"No. But, they will. We're sure of that!"

I tried to speak quietly but authoritatively. "We need to have everything in writing from the government."

"Don't worry, Sammy. They will give it."

I agreed to move forward with the fulfillment of their dream. They organized ushers, and counselors, and rented a sound system for the stadium. Everything went well. They called me again in August and told me they had permission from the sports federation for the stadium and the publicity was strong in the city.

I again asked, "But what about the government permission?"

"We've spoken to them, and they have promised to give it. They are in the process of having all the necessary officials sign the documents. They told us that we could pick them up between September 10th and 15th. Some officials have already signed them."

I was concerned that we would only receive the documents one month before the event. Yet, their enthusiasm and faith convinced me of my need for patience. I would soon travel to Brazil for a major evangelistic event and was scheduled to arrive back in the United States on September 11, 2001 – in time to call Sudan the next day to find out about the permits. Meanwhile, our friends from Egypt would go into the country and train counselors for the meeting. Also, a Rwandan colleague would travel to Sudan the evening of September 11th to assist with the organizational needs.

As I boarded the late evening flight on September 10, 2001 from Rio de Janeiro to the United States, I thought about my friends in Sudan and quietly prayed for them. "Oh, God, please be with them. Give them wisdom. Help them to not be discouraged if they don't receive the permission." I wanted to rebuke myself for my lack of faith.

Shortly after going through immigration and customs in the DFW airport the next morning, I watched televisions broadcasting scenes of an airplane flying into the Twin Towers in New York City. It wasn't long before another one became a weapon of the terrorists. Within a few minutes of the attacks, the Dallas/Fort Worth airport looked like a ghost town. My wife, Tex, and I hurriedly rented a vehicle to drive the remainder of the way home.

As we drove, I knew the world had changed dramatically. A deep darkness had been released. The shadowy evil was no longer in some far away place, but mysterious clouds had ushered darkness on to the shores of America. When we stopped to fill our vehicle with gas, the store manager's eyes were filled with shock. I was surprised when this total stranger asked, "Is this the end of the world?"

My thoughts filled with concern for my colleagues in Sudan. Did they know what had happened? How would this tragedy affect our plans? Confusion reigned during the next few days. I quickly learned that my Egyptian friends had made it out of the country before the attack took place in New York City, but my Rwandan colleague had a different experience. His flight from Kenya was almost to Khartoum when the pilot announced, "We will be returning to Nairobi."

When I spoke with my Sudanese friends, they were insistent on continuing with the plans. "If we don't go forward, they will crush us. It's important that you come." Their courage inspired me, but my fears crippled me. Friends and colleagues in the U.S. cautioned me, "Sammy, you need to cancel the meetings. You can't go. It's too dangerous."

After I released the other team members from their commitments to travel with me, I went to a place where I often talk with my Father. It's a place under a cluster of trees, where my tears have often watered the ground. I paced for at least a half an hour, not knowing what to say. Once I was able to speak, I felt like a volcano had erupted within my soul. "Oh, God, help! I don't know what to do. I'm afraid! I don't want to die, but I don't want to forsake my friends in Sudan." I fell to my knees and covered my face, weeping.

After several minutes, peace slowly rose in my heart. I stood, lifting my hands toward heaven. "Father, I'm willing to go, but would you send someone to travel with me?"

I returned to my home and shared my fears with my wife. She was so sweet. She said, "I'll go with you."

I chuckled. "I think I can run faster without you."

Her smile calmed my heart. I pulled her into my body and gave her a tender hug. "I'm willing to go. But I feel like I need someone to go with me. I don't think there's anyone who would do that."

The doorbell rang as I finished sharing my heart. Once our son, Dave, entered, he said, "Well, I guess you've cancelled the trip to Sudan."

I stared at the floor. "No, I feel I should go."

"Who's going with you?"

"Right now, no one."

A smile crawled across his face. "I'd like to go. The students in our ministry had an all night prayer meeting last night, and God placed a deep burden in our hearts for Sudan. I think God may want me to go with you."

We discussed the difficulties of getting a visa and finding flights into Sudan at this late stage, but decided to attempt it. Dave and his wife, Kelly, prayed and were in agreement that he should go. A pastor from Georgia also decided to go with us. Three Brazilian cameramen also committed to go with us. A few days before we left for Sudan, Sudanese pastors let me know that official documents from the government had been given them.

The arrival in Khartoum was filled with joy and concern. The faces of the pastors greeting us at the airport showed incredible enthusiasm. Yet their eyes revealed the anxiety residing deep within. They had hired a team of Christian security guards. When we arrived at the hotel, they wouldn't allow me to enter the room until they had searched every nook in the quarters.

When we traveled to the stadium, they placed the vehicles in which our teams were traveling in the middle of a motorcade. Security guards rode in front of and behind us. It all seemed surreal. I was shocked when we arrived at the stadium. Many thousands, perhaps 20,000 people, had gathered to hear the message of Christ in this Islamic land. I preached with all of my heart, while two large security guards stood on each side of me. When I gave the invitation for people to follow Jesus, I almost broke down weeping.

A cloud of dust rose as thousands of Sudanese made their way to the front of the platform to pray with me. I saw tears in many of their eyes as I led them in a prayer of repentance and faith in Jesus. God had proved Himself faithful. When we returned to the hotel, we prayed together and gave thanks for God's faithfulness. I wondered what would happen in the coming days. Normally, the first day of such evangelistic events has the smallest attendance.

It was difficult to fall asleep that night. Loud banging on my door awakened me early the next morning. Several pastors were waiting in the hall. Something was wrong. Within the next few minutes, I was faced with a major decision – bow to the fear that had plagued me or reach deep into my soul and grab the courage, which only God could give.

The pastors described what had taken place. The light that had penetrated the stadium the previous day had dispelled a large area of darkness and the thick blackness screamed with vengeance. Al Qaeda and the Muslim Brotherhood threatened to bomb the stadium. The government sent troops to the stadium and surrounded it, preventing anyone from entering. They issued an order to cancel the remaining worship services.

I asked the pastors their thoughts about what we should do. They already had a plan. One of them said, "We must not stop, but it's impossible to continue with the meetings. We will call all the pastors in the city together, and we want you and your team to speak to them about spiritual revival. We will take a different approach. We can't have the stadium, but we want you to light a fire in our hearts that will spread throughout the city and nation. Are you willing to do that?"

"Yes, of course."

"There's one other thing you need to consider before you give a final answer. We will have all the Christian leaders in the city in one place. If Al Qaeda and the Muslim Brotherhood want to destroy the leadership of the Christian church, they will have an easy target. Anyone who comes to the meetings must be willing to die. If you and your team decide to participate, you must be willing to sacrifice your lives. Otherwise, you should not come."

I took a deep breath and swallowed hard. "Let me talk to the team today and pray with them. I'll give you my final answer this afternoon."

My heart was heavy as I called the team together. I knew they had come with me at great risk to their lives. I couldn't make the decision for them. They had to make it, and they might be making a choice of life or death. The responsibility weighed heavy on my heart. I loved and appreciated the Brazilians and my friend from

Georgia. My own son's life was hanging in the balance. We spent time in prayer and then made our decision. It didn't come easily. But ultimately everyone decided to participate in the meetings.

I don't know that I've ever seen such hunger and thirst for God as I saw in that first meeting with the Christian leadership in Khartoum. God's Spirit fell powerfully. Tears flowed freely. Courage rose rapidly. The Christian leaders determined to never give up, but acted even more boldly. After one of the services, they came to me with some unexpected news. "We've set up a meeting for you to meet with the Vice President of the nation."

Our team spent time in prayer that night. We traveled the next day with the key leadership of the Christian community to meet the Vice President. When we arrived, not only was the Vice President present, but the Chief of Staff for the President was also there. After formal introductions, the two Sudanese leaders made opening remarks. I looked closely into the eyes of the pastors and saw courage. It was contagious. I knew what I needed to do. I not only needed to plead the case for these persecuted Christians, but I had to share the gospel with the political leadership of Sudan. They may never otherwise have the opportunity to hear of God's love found in Jesus.

My life was never the same after spending a week with these leaders living under a thick cloud of darkness. I learned much about courage from these faith-filled women and men. I learned that courage is not a natural way of life when darkness surrounds us. It's a supernatural gift of life that flows from the One who is light. I learned several lessons from those living in a dark world during a very dark time.

First, darkness can roar, but it can't destroy. It often shouts, causing us to shudder, but God's love chases it away, leaving us a peace that passes all human understanding. When fear approaches, we must immediately run into the arms of God – the place where we find shelter in the storm.

Not only does prayer produce peace in the darkness, but it is also the priority of the church. When we study the New Testament, we find a pattern, which not only produces peace but also enables the church to expand. That pattern becomes a model for developing courage. A summary of this model can be found in Acts 4:31. The early church was birthed in a prayer meeting. They continually sought God. They drew near to God, and He drew near to them. Next, they were filled with the Holy Spirit. The fullness of the Holy Spirit produced both courage and character. When courage and character unite, they produce an incredible effulgence of God's glory. Darkness is dispelled. Light shines. Nothing is impossible.

Because of the empowering of the Holy Spirit, Christians spoke the word of God with great boldness. The church grew rapidly in very dark times. They added 3,000 members to the church, then more. Ultimately, the word of God was multiplied. Leaders like Paul were arrested and later killed. Most of the Apostles were murdered for courageously proclaiming Christ. Later, many were burned on stakes. Yet no government could stop the church; no philosophical movement could hinder its growth; no religious group could prevent its rise.

Al Qaeda, ISIS, and The Muslim Brotherhood,– all creep about in today's dark shadows. They threaten our way of life. If we're not careful, they may produce such fear that our hearts tell us to run and hide. But I've witnessed believers who live in that darkness, and it hasn't been able to destroy them. It has only caused the light to be seen more clearly. The light within our hearts has dispelled the darkness surrounding us. It has released the glory of God. It has produced men and women of Christ-like character.

The light of men and women of godly character shines. It's the same light that has shined brightly during the days of the past Great Awakenings in the Western world. If we return to our roots, the same light will dispel today's approaching darkness. That light is the only hope for Western civilization in this dark hour. We must never forget the words God spoke to Joshua. "Have I not commanded you? Be strong and courageous. Do not be frightened, and do not be dismayed, for the Lord your God is with you wherever you go" (Joshua 1:9 ESV).

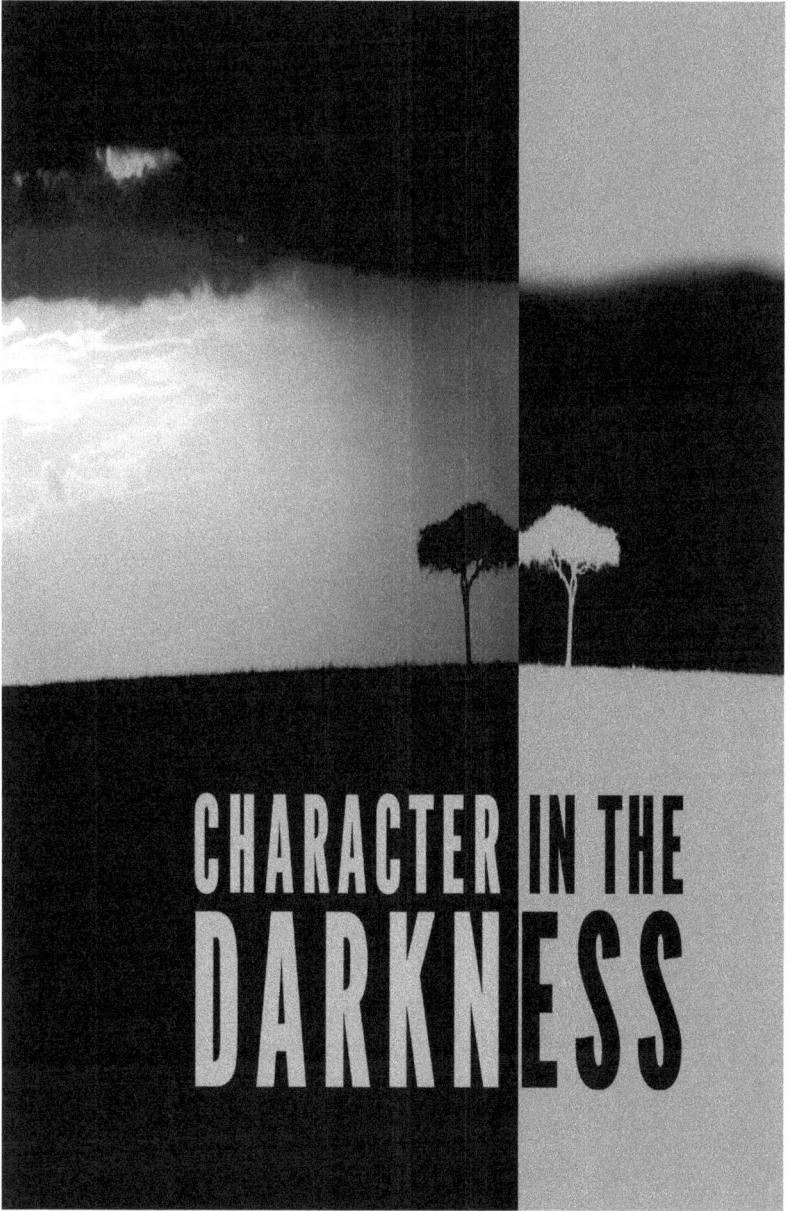

CHARACTER IN THE DARKNESS

Chapter 5
Character in the Darkness

Character shines brightest when the night is darkest, and it displays its beauty when we are at our weakest. Character defies our attempts to become passive. It grows or withers, but refuses to become stagnant. Character has the ability to grow in any environment, but excels when the winds of adversity blow, the rains of weaknesses fall, and the floods of evil rise. Character shines in such storms.

My international ministry began during a storm that threatened to extinguish the light of freedom for all mankind. The red storm had risen over Eastern Europe and posed great danger to Christians. Dictators in communist-controlled Eastern Europe closed churches, jailed followers of Jesus, and attempted to silence those who secretly lit the candle of faith. During those days, I was introduced to some of the most beautiful people I'd ever meet. The light shining deeply in their hearts produced an effulgence of God's glory and Christ-like character. Their light would eventually dispel the darkness in the region.

It was at that time I came to understand the power of the partnership between character and prayer. When the two work in concert, they have the ability to tear down Iron Curtains and open human hearts to the love of God. The splendor and beauty of those two partners caused hundreds of thousands of citizens to sing in the streets and shout on top of fallen walls. Together, they accomplished the impossible, causing atheists to cry out, "There is a God! There is a God!"

God used two men in Eastern Europe during the days of darkness. Both displayed Christ-like character and were humble men of prayer. One lived in East Germany, and the other in Romania. They never met one another, but each developed a secret place of prayer during the early 1970s. Both came to the same conclusion: *God's work must be done in complete dependence upon Him, and it must be done by men and women of character.*

❧

Light in East Germany's Darkness

The gentleman in East Germany lived through two generations of persecution. As a Lutheran minister, Pastor Busch had been imprisoned under Hitler's regime because he refused to "Heil Hitler." After World War II, the communists wouldn't permit him to pastor because he refused to go along with the party line that said communism held the hope for the world. When I first met him, he reminded me of my father; tall and strong, yet quiet and humble. Suffering for his faith had produced an inward beauty, a warm light that protected his heart from the surrounding darkness.

Pastor Busch lived in a small apartment in East Berlin. Most people probably thought of this senior adult as a person with a boring life, only waiting for death to knock at his door. The government certainly couldn't fathom the incredible power dwelling deep within him. I met the old pastor after a time of ministry in West Berlin.

It wasn't difficult to see the spiritual darkness prevalent during those days. West Berlin was free, and the city was colorful and well lit. East Berlin was bland, dangerous, and dark. Crossing from West Berlin into East Berlin was like lifting your foot to take a step at high noon, but when your foot touched the ground, it had turned to midnight. East Berlin was encircled by a wall, which kept people from escaping to freedom. Machine gun towers were strategically placed every 200 yards. The East German soldiers were trained to kill their fellow countrymen if they attempted to escape.

The church suffered greatly during that period. Young people were forced to make a decision at the age of fourteen—to be a part of the communist "Freie Deutsche Jugend" (Free German Youth) or a part of the church. If they chose the church, they lost their educational and economic future. Consequently, young people fled the church en masse.

The elderly pastor wanted us to understand the situation and took my wife and me to an old, beautifully constructed church. I was broken-hearted at what I witnessed. Only a handful of older people attended services. It appeared the communists had achieved their goal. A generation of Christians had lost their way in the darkness. The situation was so dire that one Lutheran pastor, so distraught over the loss of an entire generation, poured gasoline over himself and lit a match. The darkness seemed impenetrable to him. But it wasn't to Pastor Busch who had suffered under Hitler. He had learned the secret of overcoming darkness in the midst of suffering.

Pastor Busch prayed. Even though he wasn't allowed to minister in any public manner, he committed himself to developing Christ-like character. Hitler couldn't destroy his dreams, the communists couldn't stop his faith, and the present darkness couldn't douse the flame burning deep within. He continued praying and living in a quiet and humble manner. Men of darkness thought they had destroyed his light, but they were wrong.

As we left East Berlin, Pastor Busch brought us to what he called the *Temple of Tears*. It was the spot where relatives from the west parted from their East Berlin families as they headed to the other side of the wall. It was hard to leave the old man. He hugged and kissed us, and our eyes filled with tears. He looked up at the towers. "Maybe someday I will be able to visit you on the other side."

I smiled. "I hope so."

We left him, knowing we had been with someone who walked humbly with God, lived by faith, and refused to give up the dream of reaching a new generation for Christ. But I couldn't shake the emotions I experienced in East Berlin; the grayness of the streets and the constant feeling of oppression, contrasted with the kindness and courage of an aged pastor.

We returned to the United States. It was nearly a year before we were able to return to East Berlin. When we arrived at Pastor Busch's home, he heartily embraced us and wept. He told us how he had prayed for us since we had last met. Then he spoke of the impossible. "I want you to pray about returning next summer. East Berlin will host 100,000 elite communist youth from every communist-dominated country in the world. You must infiltrate them and tell them of the love of Jesus."

"That would be impossible!"

The old man's lip curled upward and his eyes sparkled. "Yes, it will be impossible for you, but not for God."

My mouth dropped as I stood in front of a man whose life had been molded by suffering and persecution. He was kind yet courageous, bold but prayerful, and full of faith in God and love for a new generation of East German youth. Because I stood in front of a man of Christ-like character I couldn't dismiss his seemingly impossible dream. His character forced me to consider returning to share Jesus with 100,000 committed communist youth.

God brought two friends and me back to East Berlin for the communist youth festival the following summer. We infiltrated the meeting and led more than 200 hardcore atheistic youth to Christ. In the next section, *God's Glory in the Darkness*, I describe in detail the incredible story of God's work in that meeting. Those who became followers of Jesus lived in different countries, most of them in Eastern Europe. My friends and I later contacted those who made commitments to Christ, and it thrust us into a ministry behind "The Iron Curtain." That ministry lasted from the mid-1970s until the end of 1989, when the Berlin Wall came down.

We witnessed thousands of young people coming to Christ in one of the darkest regions of the world. Most people have heard of the political figures instrumental in the collapse of communism, but few have heard of the humble men of character who prayed and dreamed of that day. They were the grassroots people who kept the light shining in the darkness. Because their character had been molded by fire, no government could snuff out the light, especially not of people like Pastor Busch.

God used people of Christ-like character to sow the seeds that grew into a nation's transformation. An entire generation became courageous because of a prayer movement. I describe the East German youth revival that shook the nation in the next section, *God's Glory in the Darkness*. World history was changed. A nation was impacted by a few humble, praying people.

ҩ

The Light Shines in Romania

Many observers say that the darkest nation among the Warsaw Pact countries during the days of communism was Romania. Nicolae Ceaușescu, Romania's dictator, persecuted Christians more severely than any of his communist counterparts. The persecution was so severe that Dr. David Funderbirk, U.S. Ambassador to Romania under Ronald Reagan's presidency, resigned his post in protest of Ceaușescu's tyranny.

However, the dictator's hideous darkness couldn't eradicate God's light. About the same time that Pastor Busch sought God on behalf of a generation of East German youth, a Romanian pastor lit a candle in his country that eventually brought light to the entire nation. Some of his parishioners described him as "a godly man." Others said that he was a "man of prayer." But most agreed that he was God's instrument to light the match that caused fire from heaven to spread throughout the nation.

During the mid-1970s, Pastor Liviu Olah taught the people in his congregation to pray in an unusual manner. "Ask God to allow us to preach in the stadiums of the nation. Pray that we will be able to tell people about Jesus on television and radio."

Some protested. "Pastor, don't you understand? We lose our jobs because of our faith. Some of us have been beaten because of our love for Jesus. Others have gone to prison, and some have even been killed. That would be impossible!"

Pastor Liviu responded with the same quiet courage as the East German pastor. "Yes, it may be impossible with men, but all things are possible with God."

Pastor Liviu—a man full of faith, a pastor with courage, and a person of Christ-like character—challenged the Christians in the northwestern region of Romania to seek God for a mighty outpouring of His Spirit.

He took two actions that caused the light to spread throughout the nation and produce one of the greatest displays of God's glory in the 20th century. He not only called the people in his congregation to prayer, but he also called them to repentance. Evangelical Christians were called *Repenters* during those days. It was a derogatory term used to chastise followers of Christ. However, Pastor Liviu wore it as a badge of honor. He believed that Christ truly changed people when they followed Him. Thus, they were *Repenters*. When he lit the candle that spread throughout the nation, it wasn't through a message to the communists. It was because of a message he gave to followers of Jesus. He preached, "The *Repenters* must repent!" He knew the great power to shatter the darkness was found in the character of the people. He knew the hope wasn't as much in attacking the darkness surrounding them, but rather destroying the darkness within them.

A few years ago, Christians in Romania sent me a copy of the message he preached on a night in which he called for repentance. During the days of communism, people brought tape recorders to church and hid them in their bags and purses. On that night, someone had secretly taped his message. Pastor Liviu spoke of the darkness in their culture and the need for God's people to repent. Because the person taping the message sat in the congregation, you could hear persons near him/her weeping. As Pastor Liviu continued preaching, the cries grew louder. It became so loud that he was forced to shout over the noise. Then the wailing became so thunderous that it completely drowned out his voice. The *Repenters* repented! I was so overwhelmed as I listened to the recording that I placed my head in my hands and wept.

The church grew and became one of the largest Evangelical churches on the continent of Europe. There was something very interesting about their experience. The church had entered into *A Covenant of Repentance*. Even though the church would have considered itself a good church at the time, they felt like they had conformed to the culture rather than to Christ.

One example could be found in their work habits. Under communism, no one had an incentive to work. It didn't matter how hard one worked, their pay remained the same. Without monetary incentive, people had no reason to excel. The system stole people's ability to improve their lives, and factories broke down. It was a major economic reason for the collapse of communism.

Christians fell into the trap of adopting the habits of the darkness. Instead of using the full potential of their skills and abilities, they acted and worked like everyone else. When Pastor Liviu called for repentance, the situation changed. Christians became the best workers in the factories. Their communist bosses, who were also their persecutors, respected them. Their work ethic reflected their character, and it became the light in the darkness. Communists came to Christ. Persecutors of Christianity became proponents of the gospel. A fire was lit that would later bring light to the nation. It was one of the most amazing moments of spiritual awakening in modern history. An entire nation was transformed. A revolution erupted.

What the news media failed to report when the revolution transpired was that the theme song during the revolution was a song about the second coming of Christ. Suffering Christians were at the forefront of the nation's transformation. They didn't fight with military weapons, but with spiritual ones. They were shot and many killed by Ceauşescu's Securitate (Secret Police) in Timisoara, one of the nation's larger cities. Yet, they overcame.

They conquered through prayer. An entire nation was awakened. I describe this historical display of the light of God's glory more fully in the next section, *God's Glory in the Darkness*.

❧

Character: the platform from which the light shines

The fire in Romania and East Germany that shocked the world spread because it found hearts willing to change. God's fire spreads in the darkest places when it finds people longing to grow in Christ-like character more than anything else they desire in life. Character development may be the most important thing a person does to thwart the spread of darkness.

Christians may wonder how we could have any impact on groups like ISIS or Al Qaeda. The answer is simple. The secret to defeating the darkness from without is in allowing the light within to dispel the inner darkness of our own lives. The inner light becomes the platform for overcoming the global darkness and the darkness down the street. When the church awakens to the power source deep within, she will discover there's no situation too difficult. If the church in the West would allow God's light to shine through a commitment to grow in Christ-like character, she could transform the Western world. The hope is closer than we could ever imagine. It lies in our own hearts. When we allow God to change us, we build a platform for nations to change. But first, the *Repenters* must repent!

Character builds credibility, which becomes the platform from which we proclaim the gospel. There's never been a time in history when the gospel has had a greater human and technological platform than today. We have Christian radio, television, blogs, social media, websites, and a multitude of other platforms for people to hear our voices. However, none of those platforms have been able to halt the rapidly spreading darkness. There's nothing wrong with utilizing those platforms if we realize they have been created to make our voices heard. However, what brings revival to a nation is not the thunder of our voices, but the authenticity of our faith. The old time revivalists called it holiness. A holy life is simply one that has been set apart for God's glory. Authenticity doesn't mean perfection. It means there's a genuine attempt to **grow** in Christ-likeness. Our hearts belong to Jesus, and we long to grow into His image. Grow is the operative word.

Many people confuse maturity with Christian growth. A person cannot become mature in her faith without growing in Christ-likeness. But a person can become mature in her faith and cease growing. Developing Christ-like character is an ongoing, life-long process. There's no plateau a person reaches where she can say, "Ah, I've arrived." One of the great problems facing the church today is that many have grown in their faith but have become satisfied with their level of maturity. It has left the church lethargic in a critical moment of history. A revived Christian is a growing Christian. Revival accelerates the growth process, and it resets a heart that has grown stagnant.

One reason we must continue to grow in Christ-like character throughout our lives is because of our vulnerabilities. All of us have "blind spots"—areas in our lives that others see easily, but are difficult for us to recognize because of the darkness hiding them. These blind spots leave us vulnerable, and they often render us powerless at the very moment God wants to work the greatest. The blind spots become apparent when God's light shines brightest, but are also hidden when darkness is permitted to dwell in our hearts. These "blind spots" steal from the authenticity of our faith and keep us from becoming like Christ. That's why the prayer of our hearts must continually be, "Search my heart, Oh God." Blind spots are exposed during what the Bible describes as "seasons of refreshing."

Billy Graham stands out as one of the great modern-day heroes of the Christian faith. One of the reasons that God has used Dr. Graham is the credibility he established over a lifetime. His integrity has been a hallmark of his ministry. He and his colleagues did something early in his ministry that enabled him to deal with the vulnerabilities of a traveling evangelist. In 1948, they established what became known as the *Modesto Manifesto*.

The North Carolina magazine, *Our State,* carried an article about Billy Graham, which was written by Jimmy Tomlin at: http://www.ourstate.com/billy-graham/. Tomlin wrote about the manifesto and its impact on Graham's ministry, stating, "That decision was made in 1948—when the young, hellfire preacher's ministry began to catch on nationwide — at a meeting with three of his ministry team members in Modesto, California. Concerned that scandal could ruin his reputation and dilute his message of salvation, Graham and his colleagues came up with the so-called 'Modesto Manifesto,' an unwritten guide for maintaining integrity—financial and otherwise—in Graham's ministry. Of the points they agreed on, the best known is Graham's refusal from that point forward to travel, meet, or eat alone with any woman other than his wife, Ruth, to avoid even the appearance of sexual impropriety."

The manifesto may seem legalistic to many today, but it was simply Reverend Graham's way of recognizing his vulnerabilities as a traveling evangelist and dealing with them. He knew that his platform for spreading the light was found in his character. Tomlin concluded his article by writing, "Some people may find such precautions prudish or extreme, but you can't argue with the results.

"There was never even a hint of scandal," says Ken Garfield, former religion editor of The Charlotte Observer, who covered Graham for 12 years and interviewed him personally. "Never a hint, and it's because he was very intentional about that."

God works through people—ordinary people. He used Thomas, a doubter; Peter, a fisherman; and Matthew, a tax collector. He still uses common ordinary people. He'll take a country boy from North Carolina named Billy Graham and give him one of the largest platforms in the history of Evangelical Christianity. The platform from which we shatter the darkness is character. All of the above have had their own spiritual issues, but they allowed God to mold them. They set up a protection around their hearts. They set their lives in a direction of growing in Christ-like character. They failed. Yes, many times. But it's difficult to doubt the authenticity of their faith.

God is looking for imperfect men and women who have set out on a journey of giving themselves wholeheartedly to Him. The Bible says, "For the eyes of the Lord run to and fro throughout the whole earth, to give strong support to those whose heart is blameless toward him" (2 Chronicles 16:9 ESV). When God finds such authenticity, He will accomplish far beyond anything we could ever imagine!

The question becomes, "How then do we grow in Christ-like character?" Perhaps the prophet Zechariah revealed the secret when he wrote, "'Not by might nor by power, but by My Spirit,' says the LORD of hosts" (Zechariah 4:6 ESV).

Chapter 6
The Holy Spirit and Character

The greatest challenges we face don't come from walls erected by atheistic regimes, nor from evil dictators with goals of exterminating Christians. The biggest tests confronting us are the spiritual walls deep within our own hearts and the evil dictator that seeks to steal, kill, and destroy our journey with God and our relationships with others. Those enemies are far greater than the one that Pastor Liviu faced and much more exasperating than the former situation in East Germany. The inner darkness stands as the greatest obstacle to overcome in order to experience God's glory.

In the previous chapter, we saw how Pastors Busch and Liviu direct us in the way of triumph. The greatness of God's love and power enables us to prevail over the most impossible circumstances. As the Scriptures say, "Little children, you are from God and have overcome them, for He who is in you is greater than he who is in the world" (1 John 4:4 ESV). Christians were facing difficult circumstances when that passage was written. But God's Word assured them that they could overcome those who opposed and persecuted them. However, many of us focus on our circumstances and fix our gaze on our failures. We quickly become distraught over our inability to live in the manner in which we know God desires.

We should realize that we're not the first to feel that way. Great men and women in the past have had to deal with the same emotions. Arguably, one of the greatest Christians in history was the Apostle Paul. He wrote, "For I do not understand my own actions. For I do not do what I want, but I do the very thing I hate.... For I know that nothing good dwells within me, that is, in my flesh. For I have the desire to do what is right, but not the ability to carry it out" (Romans 7:15, 18 ESV). Paul understood the impossibility of becoming like Jesus. He longed for such a life, but knew he couldn't achieve it with his own power. Thankfully, Paul doesn't conclude his writing by leaving us hopeless. He continues, "Wretched man that I am! Who will deliver me from this body of death? Thanks be to God through Jesus Christ our Lord" (Romans 7:24, 25 ESV).

The believability of the Bible is rooted in its audacious transparency. One of the most effective proponents of the gospel wrote frankly about his failures and needs. The substance of the gospel lies in the reality of the bad news. We are helpless to please God in our own power. It's impossible to live in the manner God expects. That's the first half of the good news. The second half is *great* news. When Paul came to the end of his abilities, he then realized the place of true victory and said, "I thank God through Jesus Christ our Lord!"

The starting place for developing Christ-like character is transparency. It's only when we're willing to admit that we can't be the light God wants us to become that we put ourselves in a position to shine brightly. Light shattering the darkness isn't some unattainable reality. It's not limited to people like Pastors

Busch and Liviu Olah. That light is available to an abused wife, a defeated teenager, and an alcoholic father. It's available to you, no matter how defeated you may feel. There's no need to cover up your failures. God is still on His throne and waiting to pour out His Spirit upon all who call upon Him in honesty and humility. We must realize that the darkness we face is deeply spiritual, and the solution is also profoundly spiritual.

இ

Confession of Sin

We take the first step to develop Christ-like character by becoming so transparent that we allow the Holy Spirit to search our hearts and expose any thought patterns, attitudes, and/or actions that have been hidden in the dark closets of our hearts. Just as in the case of Romania, deep confession of sin has always been at the beginning of any great movement of God's Spirit. If we're to experience that kind of move of the Holy Spirit in this generation, we must allow Him to have access to every secret place in our hearts. As we watch the darkness of terrorism in the global community roll onto the shores of the Western world, our light must shine brightly. Truth can defeat error. Love can conquer hate. Light always dispels darkness.

The situation we face today is similar to what transpired during the late 1960s and early 1970s. The United States was engaged in a seemingly endless war. Moral values were turned upside down as young people "turned on, tuned in, and dropped out." A psychedelic drug culture emerged in the late '60s that transformed society and changed thousands of young people. It appeared a generation had been lost.

However, something very quiet yet extraordinarily revolutionary took place at a small Methodist college outside of Lexington, Kentucky. It halted a tidal wave of darkness in the land. Dr. Dennis Kinlaw, president of the school, traveled to Canada on February 3, 1970. When he arrived at his hotel, the clerk told him, "I have an emergency note for you." When Dr. Kinlaw saw the note was from the Dean of the College, he called immediately.

Dr. Kinlaw was surprised at the Dean's first words: "I have a problem and don't quite know how to handle it…. The morning chapel isn't over yet."

Dr. Kinlaw quickly asked, "What do you mean it's not over? It's seven o'clock at night!"

The Dean explained to Dr. Kinlaw what had transpired. The Dean had been scheduled to speak that morning at chapel. He shared a testimony and then opened it for students to share. They shared what God had been doing in their lives. About five minutes before the chapel concluded, a philosophy professor turned to the Dean and said, "God is here. If you give an invitation, there will be a response." He was right. The Dean invited people to come to the altar at the front of the chapel and to seek God, asking Him to change their lives. There was a response so great that the chapel service lasted for seven days and seven nights!

A format emerged from the chapel service. A student would share a testimony of how God had dealt with him about sin in his life. Students shared how they had repented and experienced God's forgiveness and restoration. They shared how God met the needs of their hearts. When one student spoke, the light that shone from that life would rapidly penetrate the darkness in other students. They found themselves at the altar, confessing and repenting of sin. They prayed and sought God. Then came singing and the worship of God. That was followed by more testimonies.

When Dr. Kinlaw returned to Asbury, he found God's presence filling the campus. As he sat in chapel, a student came and knelt next to the seat where he sat and asked, "Dr. Kinlaw, can I talk with you?" She looked up at the school's president and said, "Dr. Kinlaw, I'm a liar. I lie so much that I don't even know when I'm lying. I'm a liar, but what do I do?"

Dr. Kinlaw gave an interesting response to the young lady. "Why don't you go back to the last person you remember lying to? Confess it to that person and ask that person's forgiveness."

She told him, "Oh, that would kill me."

"No. It would probably cure you."

Three days later the student came to Dr. Kinlaw and told him, "I'm free. I've just gone to my 34th person and confessed my sin, and I'm free!"

Students had numerous testimonies similar to this one. (This testimony of Dr. Kinlaw's was taken from YouTube at: https://www.youtube.com/watch?v=q6GPMBSbiEE.)

I spoke at Asbury College not long after the revival swept through the campus. As a result, I came in contact with many people whose lives had been changed by this move of God's Spirit. A few months later, I was speaking in Maryland, and I met a young man who had been a drug dealer who was now sharing his faith with young people on drugs. The revival from Asbury had spread to a Church of God college in Anderson, Indiana. The drug dealer went to one of the meetings, and God captured his heart, setting him free from his drug habit. He travelled to Maryland with a music group from the Church of God college. The light spread rapidly around the nation, especially to other Christian campuses. Students from Asbury went to churches and schools and shared what God had done. As they shared how the light had dispelled the darkness in their hearts, God moved throughout the audiences to whom they spoke.

Some of these Methodist students spoke one morning at chapel at Southwestern Baptist Theological Seminary, the world's largest Baptist seminary. Gary Maroney, one of my college buddies, was present that day. God grabbed Gary's heart and wouldn't let go. He was broken before the Lord, confessed, and repented of sin. I hadn't seen Gary in several years, but when we were reunited, it was obvious that something deep and lasting had taken place. He shared some things about our college days I didn't know.

When we were in college, we often filled our free time with pickup basketball games. In one of those games, I attacked the basket for a layup and accidently flung an elbow into Gary's nose. It started bleeding, and he left the game. I didn't know what had happened. But the break in Gary's nose was so bad that he had to have surgery to repair it. He became embittered toward me. However, when the students from Asbury arrived, God's light shone in the dark places of Gary's heart. He confessed his bitterness, and God set him free. When we met again, he asked my forgiveness.

I was overwhelmed and asked his forgiveness for having injured him. Gary was a different man. He and I then developed a great friendship that has lasted for decades. He has traveled with me more than any other person to the dark and difficult places in the world. When God arrives, lives are transformed. Character is developed. Relationships are restored. The light spreads more rapidly than anyone could imagine.

❦

The Empowering of the Holy Spirit

One of the students at Asbury shared, "The Holy Spirit came and watered the dry plains of my soul.... I found the secret of a victorious life, and I didn't have to spend another day without the reality of Jesus Christ in my life and without the power of the Holy Spirit."

The reason God's light searches our hearts isn't simply to show us how inadequate we are, it's to gently lead us into His victory. He brings us to the place where we can echo the words of the Apostle Paul. "I thank God through Jesus Christ our Lord." The light is much more than being a good person. The light is His presence filling us. The light produces a wonderful cleansing that places us in a position to be filled with God's Spirit. His fullness enables us to overcome attitudes, habits, and wrong thought processes. The Holy Spirit makes the impossible possible.

As we allow God to search our hearts and bring cleansing, we must then yield to the Holy Spirit. We must never forget that we cannot live in the manner He expects. We desperately need His power—His filling. But we can't be full of sin and full of God. As He cleanses us, we must then appropriate His fullness. That means we allow the Holy Spirit to take complete control of our lives. When we ask Him, He fills us. When we seek Him, He reveals Himself. When we knock, He always welcomes us. That's why Jesus said to "ask, seek, and knock."

As we are filled with the Holy Spirit, we must then learn to walk in the Spirit. The fullness of the Spirit produces character qualities. The Bible identifies the fruit of the Spirit. "The fruit of the Spirit is love, joy, peace, longsuffering, kindness, goodness, faithfulness, gentleness, self-control. Against such there is no law. And those who are Christ's have crucified the flesh with its passions and desires" (Galatians 5:22, 23 ESV). As we walk in the Spirit, we grow into the likeness of Christ.

As I look back over my life, I realize that two of the most Christ-like people I've ever known I came to know at Asbury College. The first was Dr. Frank Laubach. He was called the "Apostle to the Illiterates." He was deeply concerned that poverty and illiteracy were great hindrances to world peace. He founded Laubach Literacy in 1955, and an estimated 2.7 million people in 34 developing nations have embraced his literacy methods. He may be the only American missionary whose photo has been on a U.S. postage stamp.

I met Dr. Laubach a couple of months following the outpouring of God's Spirit at Asbury College. I was leading a group of seven young people to walk across America and call for a national revival. Leaders at Asbury heard about our walk and asked me to speak on the campus. It was an amazing time. One of the most lasting memories from that event was meeting Dr. Laubach. He spent time with our small group. He was so kind. We sat at his feet and asked a multitude of questions. Some have called him a mystic. He was certainly a man of prayer. His life displayed the light of God's glory through Christ-like character. As I listened to Dr. Laubach, I knew I was sitting at the feet of a man who had walked with God. He told me that he had prayed to see an outpouring of God's Spirit as he had seen at Asbury. He said, "I'm now ready to go to be with the Lord." He died within the next couple of months. The beauty of such a Christ-like man remains embedded in my heart until this day.

The second person I met at Asbury that has displayed great Christ-like character was Dr. Kinlaw. He has had such an impact on my life that I've occasionally said, "I need to spend time with

Dr. Kinlaw." I would clear my schedule and travel to Asbury to spend a few days with this godly man. He displays a quality of character rarely seen. After spending just a short period of time with these men, I realized that they both understood the power of the Holy Spirit, and they both experienced the revival at Asbury. However, they were certainly very godly before the outpouring took place at Asbury. Both men developed Christ-like character because of their openness to the Holy Spirit and because they had walked in His fullness for many years.

God is looking for men and women whose hearts belong to Him. He's searching for those who will yield themselves completely to the Holy Spirit. When he finds such vessels, He will pour out His Spirit in ways that will transform our lives and make us more like Jesus.

Before continuing to the next chapter, I would encourage the reader to find a quiet place and spend some time alone with God. Ask Him to search your heart. When He reveals "blind spots" and things not pleasing to Him, confess them. Turn from them and ask Him to cleanse your heart. Ask Him to fill you with His Spirit, and then live daily in this manner.

Chapter 7
Forgiveness in the Darkness

When God's Spirit comes, He heals our hurts by applying the renewing oils of grace, love, and purity to our deepest wounds. He offers mercy to the guilty and grace to the offended. Both the offender and the offended experience the forgiveness of God when the Holy Spirit touches their lives. Bitterness is released and guilt removed. Hearts, homes, and entire nations are healed when God visits His people.

When His light penetrates the darkest nights, an incredible miracle takes place. Lives are transformed, and hate turns into love. Enemies work together, Christians are refreshed, families united. Personal and social relationships experience renewal.

However, the opposite is also true. Anger rises in darkness. Bitterness thunders from ominous clouds. Relationships splinter. As night arrives, the heaviness of hatred settles on human hearts. As darkness approaches, racial, ethnic, and political rage climb into relationships and divide people.

வை

Darkness in Rwanda's Genocide

A deep darkness spread rapidly across Rwanda in 1994. Tribal tensions between Hutus and Tutsis turned into unthinkable violence. It's estimated that 800,000 people were murdered between April and June of that year because of their ethnicity. It was shortly after the genocide that pastors contacted me and asked me to come to their nation. I had previously worked with Peter Kasarivu, a Ugandan pastor who had many Rwandan friends. He told me, "The nation desperately needs healing. I believe people will listen to an outside voice. Would you consider coming to minister?"

Gary Maroney and Billy Honc, two dear friends, traveled with me to Rwanda shortly after Peter's request. After an all-night flight, I told Gary and Billy, "Once we meet the pastors, let's not ask a lot of questions about the tragedy. They may be very sensitive about what transpired and not want to discuss it."

Was I ever wrong! A group of pastors met us at the airport and took us to a hotel for breakfast. They immediately started sharing stories—horrible stories—things I never imagined human beings would do to one another. It was as though the pastors' pent-up emotions exploded as they told us what had happened. They secured a room for us after breakfast and told us to try to get a couple of hours sleep before we traveled to Butare, where the national university was located.

There was no way we could rest. Once we were inside the room we could only groan. The pastors' wounds were so severe and deep that they seared our souls. The initial encounter with those men prepared us for what we would experience in Butare. Once we arrived in the town, I spoke to students at the university.

Many of them were searching for answers to the tragedy. Others were left in a state of shock. I brought a message of forgiveness, reconciliation, and healing. They responded. Many placed their faith in Jesus, and God's healing power flowed into their broken hearts.

The students asked me to speak to their professors. They said, "Many of them are very cynical and angry with God and the church. They need God to change their hearts."

Our ministry hosted a dinner for the professors on the final evening of our stay in the town. It was one of the most difficult speaking engagements I've ever accepted. The Chancellor of the National University attended as the Guest of Honor. The custom was for the Guest of Honor to speak immediately before the featured speaker. When the Chancellor stood, he spoke only a few words, but they were sharp and penetrating. He looked at me and asked, "Reverend Tippit, where was the church? Where was the church when the genocide took place?" He then took his seat.

Everyone in the room knew the answer. Some in the church had participated in the genocide. We had visited one church where the bones of the dead bodies still lay inside. I had never seen anything so horrible—the bones of people strewn around the auditorium, and their skulls lined up on a platform outside the building. People had gone to the church, thinking it was a place of safety. Instead, it became a house of horrors.

That's why the Chancellor's question was so difficult to answer. I'm sure my response didn't satisfy him. I simply said that people had conformed to their culture rather than Christ. They had heeded the call of the dark rather than walked in the hope of the light. I shared about the power of the message of the cross to change hearts and heal hurts. I was extremely discouraged when the meeting concluded. I felt I hadn't given a sufficient answer to the Chancellor's question.

One of the professors saw the disappointment in my face. He placed his hand on my shoulder and smiled. "Don't worry. Deep in his soul, he knows the truth. The only hope for the healing of our country is Christ."

I fixed my gaze on him and thanked him.

The professor's countenance became very somber. "Everyone in my family was killed during the genocide."

My stomach knotted and I hung my head. I stammered as I attempted to speak. "I'm so sorry. I... I don't know what...."

The dear professor patted my shoulder. "I have forgiven them."

I quickly glanced up. "How? How could you forgive them?"

"By the miracle of God's grace. His grace is all I have. That's the hope for our nation. You must tell everyone that the hope for healing is found in His grace."

I had lunch the next day with the mayor of the city. He had been a professor at the university when the genocide took place. As we discussed the horror of what had transpired, he told me his story. He had seven children. When the order was given to kill all the Tutsis, his neighbor, also a professor, said to him, "You'll never be able to hide your entire family. Let me take four of your children and hide them. You and your wife can take the other three and hide with them.

As we ate, the mayor put his utensils down and cleared his throat. "I thanked my neighbor and entrusted him with four of our children." A tear welled in his eye. "As soon as my neighbor arrived at his home, he called for the militia to come and kill the children."

I don't know which dropped the fastest, my fork or my mouth. I couldn't speak. Neither could he. I finally asked, "How are you handling it?"

"It's difficult. But I've forgiven him." He must have seen the perplexity on my face. "You've spoken to our students about the power of the message of the cross, and the healing of God's grace. These are not just words to me. They are life and hope."

I shook my head. "It just doesn't seem natural."

"It's not. It's supernatural."

ᘒ

Hope for a Nation

I returned to Kigali, the nation's capital, with a somber understanding of the power of forgiveness. I was so glad I had met those two men during the first part of my time in Rwanda. Seeing God's power in their lives gave me great confidence as I spoke to the leaders of the nation.

When we returned to Kigali, I spoke at a large outdoor evangelistic meeting as well as a pastors' conference and a dinner with church and political leaders. The meeting with the political leaders was one of the most unusual events in which I've participated. I believe it laid a foundation for the future of the nation.

The tension was as thick as an early morning fog when the political leaders and pastors gathered in the hotel ballroom. Pastor Leo Bukibagango, who acted as the Master of Ceremonies, opened the function in a very unusual manner. I'd never heard or seen anything like it. He welcomed the church and political leaders and then said, "Before we begin, I must first ask the political leaders to forgive us as church leaders. Some of our leaders participated in the genocide. I am so ashamed of the stain it has left on the church. On behalf of our association of pastors, we ask your forgiveness and the forgiveness of the nation."

When Pastor Leo finished his "welcome," no one knew what to say. However, the fog quickly disappeared as honest and candid conversation took place at the tables. By the time the meeting concluded, political and pastoral leaders were discussing how to bring healing to the nation.

Gary, Billy, and I concluded our time in Rwanda by leading a pastors' conference. My heart broke for these leaders. So many of them loved God dearly, but carried the burden of the atrocities that others had committed. They lived in the deepest discouragement I had ever seen among Christian leaders. The load they carried wasn't only that a few pastors had participated in the genocide that created a terrible testimony for the entire church. It was also the situations they themselves faced in many of their congregations. One pastor told me that there were two women who sat on the same bench in his church. The husband of one of woman had killed the other woman's husband. It seemed like every pastor had a similar story.

Gary, Billy, and I preached, prayed with, and ministered to these dear leaders. We shared the message of forgiveness that flows from what Jesus did when He died on the cross. As we concluded each session, we observed many of them releasing the shackles of bitterness that had held them in bondage. As forgiveness flowed into the hearts of the leaders, jubilation descended in the Presbyterian Church in the center of Kigali. I've never seen such joy erupt as what happened at the close of the final session. As we sang, everyone spontaneously broke into a dance. It was the most euphoric scene I've ever witnessed. The healing of the nation had begun with the healing of the spiritual leaders.

One might wonder what kind of long-term affect that spiritual revival had. Pastor Joseph Karasanyi was one of the organizers of the meeting that we held in Rwanda. He was interviewed for our ministry's newsletter fourteen years after the genocide. He shared about the spiritual progress in the nation. He said that Pastor Leo had started more than 60 churches, with some of them having more than 1,000 people in attendance. Pastor Joseph himself only had 20 members in his church immediately following the genocide. However, he reported that he was now overseeing 50 churches, with some having up to 1,000 in attendance.

Pastor Joseph explained that the progress in the nation was much more than church growth. He said, "People had turned away from God because of the genocide. The message of hope and forgiveness turned the hearts of the people back to God. The message was different from what they had known. Also, the government officials were affected. We now have many Christians in the Parliament and other areas of leadership. Our country is now one of the fastest developing nations in Africa. The country had been destroyed. The people had lost their confidence, their hope. No one knew how to change that. But this message changed all of that. Political and spiritual leaders were encouraged when Sammy brought both groups together for the first time after the genocide. It was the beginning of something really wonderful for our country."

☙

Two Torturers

Rwanda had traveled through one of the most terrible times of national torture in the twentieth century. The torture had its roots in intergenerational bitterness. It wasn't the first time for the country to experience horrific mass murders. Hutus and Tutsis had gone through horrible conflicts in the past. One of the problems Rwanda faced was that people had never fully dealt with the two torturers who brought about the ghastly genocide. These torturers have been around for thousands of years. They've destroyed families, ruined friendships, split churches, and started wars. Who are they? *Guilt* and *Bitterness!*

When forgiveness is not applied to guilty or broken hearts, guilt and bitterness is often passed down to future generations. Hate hangs around and the darkness engulfs the hearts of people years later. I've not only seen this phenomenon in Rwanda, but in other nations as well.

Guilt takes up residence in a person's heart when the person has a wrong attitude or violates God's law. Time doesn't remove the guilt. Time can certainly help the healing process after reconciliation has taken place, but it doesn't have the power by itself to heal. That is why confession of sin is critical to revival. Guilt lives in the dark places of our lives. Confession leads us from the night into the morning sunlight.

We need to understand that God is not only a God of grace, but He is also a just God. He doesn't wink at wrongness. There were people in Rwanda who committed horrible atrocities and had to be held accountable for those deeds. Forgiveness doesn't mean that accountability ceases. All of us will one day stand before a holy and just God and give an account for our lives—our actions and attitudes.

When we are completely honest, we must admit that we've all fallen short of God's standards. I certainly have. I've messed up—majorly, lots of times. When we confess our wrongs and turn from them, we discover grace, amazing grace. However, when we hide or deny our wrongs, guilt creeps into the deepest part of our souls and takes us captive. This torturer hides in the darkness and lures us into his shackles.

The only way to find freedom from this evil torturer is to run to the cross of Christ with a honest heart and repentant spirit. God looks for humility in our hearts. When He sees it, He bestows grace upon us. The joy of forgiveness flows, lives are changed and broken relationships mended.

There's a second torturer who seeks to destroy God's plan for our lives—bitterness. Guilt originates from what we've done wrong, but bitterness grows in the soil of a wounded heart.

After having seen the horrific aftermath of Rwanda's genocide, I have great concern for my own country. I don't think I've ever seen our nation as divided as we are today. Anger seems to be the order of the day. It's often difficult to watch two people disagree on any subject because it ends up in a shouting match. We desperately need reconciliation in our homes, communities, and among racial and ethnic groups. Reconciliation begins with honesty, and freedom from guilt flows from confession and heart-felt repentance.

Reconciliation is a two-way street. When we hurt someone or act in a wrongful manner, we must have a repentant heart that turns away from the wrong committed and depends upon God for the strength to cease the behavior.

The second part of reconciliation is forgiving those who have harmed us. Many people find this the most difficult aspect of reconciliation. Yet it's absolutely necessary if we're to escape the bondage of bitterness. We must forgive those who have wronged us. Otherwise, bitterness will take root in the deepest part of our lives and ultimately usher darkness into the inner chambers of our hearts.

It's not only difficult to forgive those who have hurt us, but often it's impossible. Some injuries are so deep that they cripple us. The worst wounds frequently come from the people we love most, and many of the hurts have their source in broken family relationships. Numerous people carry profound pain from childhood into their adult lives. The origin of a great number of broken marriages lies in the hurts inflicted during the tender years of our youth. When we harbor bitterness, we have a tendency to hide it in a dark closet of our hearts. What we don't realize is that the darkness doesn't remain dormant. It grows, and at some point in our lives, it will lash out in a very destructive manner.

Forgiving those who have hurt us is not an option if we're going to walk in the light. When Jesus taught His disciples to pray, He taught us to forgive those who had wounded us. The impossibility of His words drives us to our knees, to the place of absolute dependence upon God. That's the great lesson I learned from those professors in Rwanda. There is a place where the impossible becomes possible: the cross.

When we see forgiveness streaming from the One who was and is absolute purity, we bow in worship. We find the hope for the healing of our hurting hearts when we hear His words spoken from a cruel Roman cross, "Father, forgive them." Grace and forgiveness flow from His heart and act as medicine for our most profound wounds. Healing begins, and character is formed.

We must allow wrongs to escort us to a fresh encounter with Jesus. No one has ever been wronged the way He was. Yet, He was full of grace and forgiveness. When we take our hurts and bow before Him, His grace fills our hearts. We draw forgiveness from the well of grace He places deep within us.

Character grows because light lives in the place of forgiveness. That's how millions of people over centuries have found peace and developed character. It's a mystery to observe people in a place like Rwanda draw grace and strength from an event that took place more than 2,000 years ago. It's remarkable to watch healing flow into the deepest wounds of their hearts. The grace available for the hurting people of Rwanda is accessible to each of us. It's found at the cross, the place where Christ-like character is formed. The cross is the source of spiritual growth. It's where we find health and hope.

Great spiritual revivals occur when forgiveness flows into our hearts. Forgiveness was a major part of the Asbury revival, the awakening in Romania, and other great outpourings of God's Spirit throughout the centuries. Forgiveness brought hope to devastated lives in Rwanda. We experience revival when we look to the cross, by faith take His grace and forgiveness, and apply them to our hearts. Faith in what Jesus did on the cross is the source of developing Christ-like character.

Chapter 8
Love–God's Bright Light

It has been an interesting and exciting journey traveling into war zones and other dangerous places. I never attempted to build a strategy for reaching the difficult areas of the world. It was only as I began going to the dark and difficult places that I discovered a deep spiritual hunger for light in those regions. God broke open my heart, and doors opened around the world to reach hurting nations.

After I ministered to leaders in Rwanda, Christians in nearby Burundi and the Democratic Republic of Congo heard what God had done in Rwanda. They were going through similar situations as war raged in their communities. As darkness covered their countries, people searched for hope. They were looking for any sign of light. Hope rose in their hearts as they heard the reports from Rwanda, and they contacted me, asking me to come to their communities.

It was amazing to see the longing for hope in such dark places. We hired a pilot who would fly our team into a war zone in the Congo where Christian leaders had asked me to come. As we began our descent to land at the airport in Kisangani, the pilot spoke over the loudspeaker system, "I don't think it's safe to land. It appears that there are thousands of people at the airport. It is supposed to be closed. Something strange is happening."

We immediately prayed together as a team, asking God to protect us and show us what to do. The pilot circled the airport several times. Each time he descended a little more. He spoke again. "I don't see any fighting. We're going to land."

When we landed, an incredible surprise awaited us. People had heard that we were coming, and thousands had gathered at the airport to greet us. A band played. People sang. A group of pastors came to the plane as we exited. One of them extended his hand. "We are so happy to have you. The people have come out because it has been years since we've had any good news. Thank you for coming with good news."

We were brought immediately to the Governor's office. He told us, "Our people desperately need hope."

God moved mightily in the following days.

Yet what happened in the Congo was small compared to the light shattering the darkness in Burundi. The war in Burundi was rooted in the same Hutu/Tutsi conflict that plagued Rwanda. What I witnessed and learned about God's light shattering darkness was burned into my soul, and I'll never forget it.

It was difficult to find a pilot who would take us into the middle of the war in Burundi because of fear of being shot down. It was too dangerous to travel by car. A colleague, Mike Scalf, had preceded my arrival in the country as he prepared for our meetings. The large hotel in the capital city was completely empty. Pastor Joseph Karasanyi and Mike were their only guests. The situation was dire.

When my wife and I arrived at the airport, there was only a small band of pastors to greet us. We were taken to the hotel and told not to leave our room. Pastor Joseph said, "It's too dangerous." There had already been threats made against my life before I even arrived. My wife and I spent much time in prayer. The pastors came to the hotel early the next afternoon to bring us to the stadium. Hutus and Tutsis were fighting less than seven miles from our meeting place. The football field was packed with people from both ethnic groups waiting to hear the gospel.

They worshipped. Their singing inspired me. Their faces spoke of a longing for peace, and their search for hope could easily be seen in their eyes. As I made my opening remarks, I knew I needed to state my sole purpose in being there. I needed to be very clear that I had no political intentions. I pointed my index finger upward and proclaimed, "I've come with a message of peace and hope. God loves you! God loves your family!"

The people broke into applause. I continued, "God loves Bujumbura! God loves Burundi!" People shouted. They danced! They sang! And I continued my presentation. At the close of my message, I asked those who knew they needed a personal relationship with Christ to join me at the front of the platform and told them I would pray with them. Many hundreds responded.

When they arrived at the front of the platform they did something I had never seen. Normally, people respond by coming and standing in front of me, and I pray with them. However, these people didn't do that. They prostrated themselves on the ground, with their faces in the dirt. Their humility was deeply moving and their brokenness overwhelmed me. People wept as I prayed with them. I wept as I prayed with them! I witnessed the wonderful work of God in people's hearts.

There were television reporters at the stadium that afternoon, and they filmed everything that took place. When my wife and I returned to our hotel, we watched the evening news broadcast.

The prime time news was almost completely dedicated to our meeting.

I was awakened early the next morning. The voice on the other end of the phone said, "Pastor Tippit, this is Ambroise Niyonsaba. I'm the Cabinet Minister heading the peace committee for the government and leading the peace negotiations. We've just concluded our deliberations in Tanzania and returned to Bujumbura. I'd like to meet with you. Can you come to my office this morning?"

I quickly agreed, made myself ready, and let Joseph know what was happening. We travelled to his office. When we arrived, we were joined by a Member of Parliament from South Africa. I wasn't sure what they wanted, and it was obvious that they were edgy.

Mr. Niyonsaba folded his hands on the table and cleared his throat. "Reverend Tippit, we've just concluded our peace talks, and they failed. We've tried everything to bring the two groups together, but nothing has worked. We are not sure where to go from here. When we arrived yesterday, I was anxious to see how the media would cover our talks. However, almost all of their coverage was about your meetings."

I wasn't sure if he was upset or happy. He hadn't smiled the entire time he spoke. I kept my gaze on him as he continued.

"I couldn't believe what I saw on television. Thousands of both groups sang and danced together at the stadium. Hundreds fell to the ground and prayed together." He paused and rubbed the back of his head. "We've tried everything to bring them together. It's been impossible. It's even difficult to get leaders from both groups in the same room." He struck the table with his hand. "How are you doing it? How are you bringing them together?"

I smiled. "It's not me that has brought them together. It's God's love. It's the message of His love for all people. You will never overcome hate by negotiating people's anger and bitterness. When people come into a right relationship with God, they will love one another. If they don't, then they've found religion, not a relationship with God. Those who have come to the stadium are not searching for religion. They're searching for a genuine relationship with God. Jesus gave His life for them. He loved them, and us, before we ever thought about loving Him. When we open our hearts to Him, we're opening ourselves to the One who is perfect love. When we encounter that love, there's no room for hate. That is what has brought the people together at the stadium."

He stood, walked toward me, and extended his hand. "Would you bring this message to the entire nation?"

Unfortunately, because of the fighting, it was impossible to travel to the different regions of the country, and the war continued. However, I left Burnudi with an increased confidence in the power of the light to shatter the darkness and a deeper understanding of the nature of the light. It's the wonderful love of God that transforms darkness into light.

The ability of the light to dispel the darkness lies within the manner in which we show God's love. The Bible says that God is love. It's His nature. It's who He is. When we draw near to Him, we become like Him. Our actions reflect His nature, and we become people of Christ-like character.

The true test of our walk with God is in the way we treat one another. The Scriptures say, "At the same time, it is a new commandment that I am writing to you, which is true in Him and in you, because the darkness is passing away and the true light is already shining. Whoever says he is in the light and hates his brother is still in darkness. Whoever loves his brother abides in the light, and in him there is no cause for stumbling. But whoever hates his brother is in the darkness and walks in the darkness, and does not know where he is going, because the darkness has blinded his eyes" (1 John 2:8—11 ESV).

Those words expose the truth. Many want to say they walk in the light, but in reality, they dance with the darkness. It's easy to declare that we're walking in the light, but it's another thing to live daily with His lamp shining brightly. The only way to do that is to love others.

When Jesus was asked about the greatest commandment, He made it clear that the two greatest commandments were rooted in love. The greatest was to love God with all our hearts and the second was to love others as we love ourselves. Jesus continually spoke about a new commandment—to love one another. He even said that people would know that we are His followers by the love we have for each other. We cannot separate our love for God and our love for people from the light dwelling within us. That love is the light.

☙

Love—Three Rays of Light

The Bible gives three clear and emphatic instructions about our love for people. First: *Love one another.* There must be a radical love among Christians, one so revolutionary that people in the darkness are attracted to the light. There's not much love that flows in the darkness. Loneliness, anger, and despair lurch about the night, seeking to take captive those who walk through life without hope. When those living in despair see the kind of love that Jesus taught his followers, many will be gently drawn to the light.

However, a variety of opinions create major problems for many Christians. It often keeps us from showing the kind of love for others of which Jesus spoke. Because we are a people with deep convictions, we sometimes don't know how to respond or treat other Christians who hold another view of the Bible. Our different beliefs are often centered on minor aspects of the Scriptures. Because we don't know how to handle disagreements with others, our lights are dimmed.

I've been deeply concerned about the ability we have today to attack others who disagree with our particular points of view. It's easy to sit behind a computer and write or dictate a blog. Because it takes little effort to express our opinions, we often don't think about the affect our words will have on other Christians. I recently read of a pastors' son who committed suicide because a blogger attacked his father's credibility and then attacked the son on social media. The blogger disagreed with the pastor on a point of belief and then went for the jugular in his blogs.

The blogger probably thought he was taking a stand for his convictions, but in reality, he was attempting to fight what he believed to be darkness with darkness. We will certainly have disagreements with other Christians, but we must always treat one another with the highest degree of respect and love. When we display love for our brothers and sisters with whom we disagree, we allow God's light to shine brightly in an angry world.

Many years ago, I met a man who lived in communist-dominated Czechoslovakia. He loved God deeply and served Him with his whole heart. He had spent time in prison for his faith in Jesus. The gentleman came from a different denominational background than me. As we visited, I shared my Christian background with him. His eyes lit up and a grin came upon his face. "Oh, I was in prison with a Baptist brother! We had such sweet fellowship with one another. We encouraged and helped each other to survive during that dark time. I love that man."

When darkness surrounds us, we understand our need for one another. As we watch groups like ISIS and Al Qaeda kill and maim Christians, we must understand that this is no time to fight one another. *We* are not the enemy! The enemy is not other Christians, nor is it any other group of people. We don't need to fight among ourselves because our enemy is spiritual. The Bible tells us that our fight is not against "flesh and blood." It says that our battle is against "the cosmic powers over this present darkness, against the spiritual forces of evil in heavenly places" (Ephesians 6:12 ESV).

The historical outpourings of God's Spirit have come with a great sense of unity among God's people. Christians have put aside their differences to deal with the bigger issues. If we are to see God's glory, we must forsake our petty differences and hunger and thirst for His kingdom to come and His will to be done.

The second ray of light that emanates from God's love is *a love for others.* It doesn't matter whether they are Christians or not. Jesus said that the only commandment greater than this was to love God with all our hearts, minds, and souls. We must see people through the eyes of Jesus and love them as He loves them.

There's an interesting story in the Bible about a blind man who Jesus healed. Jesus touched him and he could see, but he saw people as trees. Jesus touched him a second time, and he saw them as human beings. I believe many Christians are like that blind man. We have been touched by God but still see incorrectly. We see people as objects and not those who have been created in God's image—people that God loves.

Darkness tags people. It gives everyone a label: Religious labels like Christian, Jew, Muslim, or Hindu. Other times it gives contrasting labels like conservative or liberal, rich or poor, black or white, and a host of other characterizations. However, we are simply God's creation. When God looks on a person, He sees someone He created, someone He loves, and someone for whom Jesus died. Jesus didn't ask whether those following him were tax collectors, fishermen, or theologians. He didn't look for their nametags. He loved as no one had ever loved. He loved a social outcast as well as a religious leader. He called and they followed. As we grow in Christ-likeness, our love for others will grow. We will see others as He sees them and love them as He loves them.

There's a third manner in which the rays of God's light shine through us: *loving those who hate us.* I've found this kind of love is the most foreign to Christians in the West. We're not familiar with persecution. Many of us grew up in a time when Christianity was a vital part of our culture. However, Western civilization has been on a slippery slope of moral and spiritual decline for the last several decades. In some areas of our culture, Christians are scorned.

Many Christians have become increasingly angry over such unkind treatment. Yet we must remember two very important facts. First, Christians around the world are suffering at a rate unknown in previous generations. There have been more Christians killed for their faith in the last thirty to forty years than have been killed in any other generation. Second, the Bible teaches that suffering is a part of our Christian lives.

The question we must answer as the night approaches is, "How do we live with darkness that attempts to destroy us?"

The answer is simple, but the application to the response is difficult. We love those who hate us. That sounds farfetched, and it is. It's impossible! Yet, that is exactly the place God wants us to live. It's in this realm we find that He is the God who specializes in the impossible. Some of the most beautiful people I've ever met are those who have suffered because of their faith. There's a genuineness about them that's produced by the Holy Spirit. They have experienced the unthinkable and discovered that God's resources are more than sufficient. They found their acceptance through the suffering of Jesus.

The greatest example of persecution can be most clearly seen when Jesus died on the cross. The One who loved perfectly was rejected by the masses. They chose to free a criminal rather than the One who had done no wrong. As He was rejected, beaten, and forsaken, He cried out, "Father, forgive them, for they know not what they do" (Luke 23:34 ESV). What love He showed to those who hated him, even to those who killed Him.

Oh, the wonder of the cross! It's at the cross that we find forgiveness. We obtain our acceptance because of His rejection. He took the punishment for our sins. He provided forgiveness. It was in His suffering that we gain the greatest gift of all, the gift of eternal life.

God has the ability to transform torture into triumph. He turns rejection into renewal. He removes hate and replaces it with love. He infuses His amazing love into our hearts and it displays the beauty and splendor of Christ. There's no greater display of Christ-like character than when we love those who hate us.

Such character chases the darkness from the lives of the hopeless. It turns the hearts of fathers to their sons and the love of mothers to their daughters. It unites families and heals hurts. It restores communities and awakens nations. A new day dawns as the Son rises in the lives of His followers. Christ-like character prepares us for a new day, one where the glory of God shines into hearts, homes, and communities. Prepare for the dawn by clothing yourself with character produced by the indwelling presence of God's Spirit.

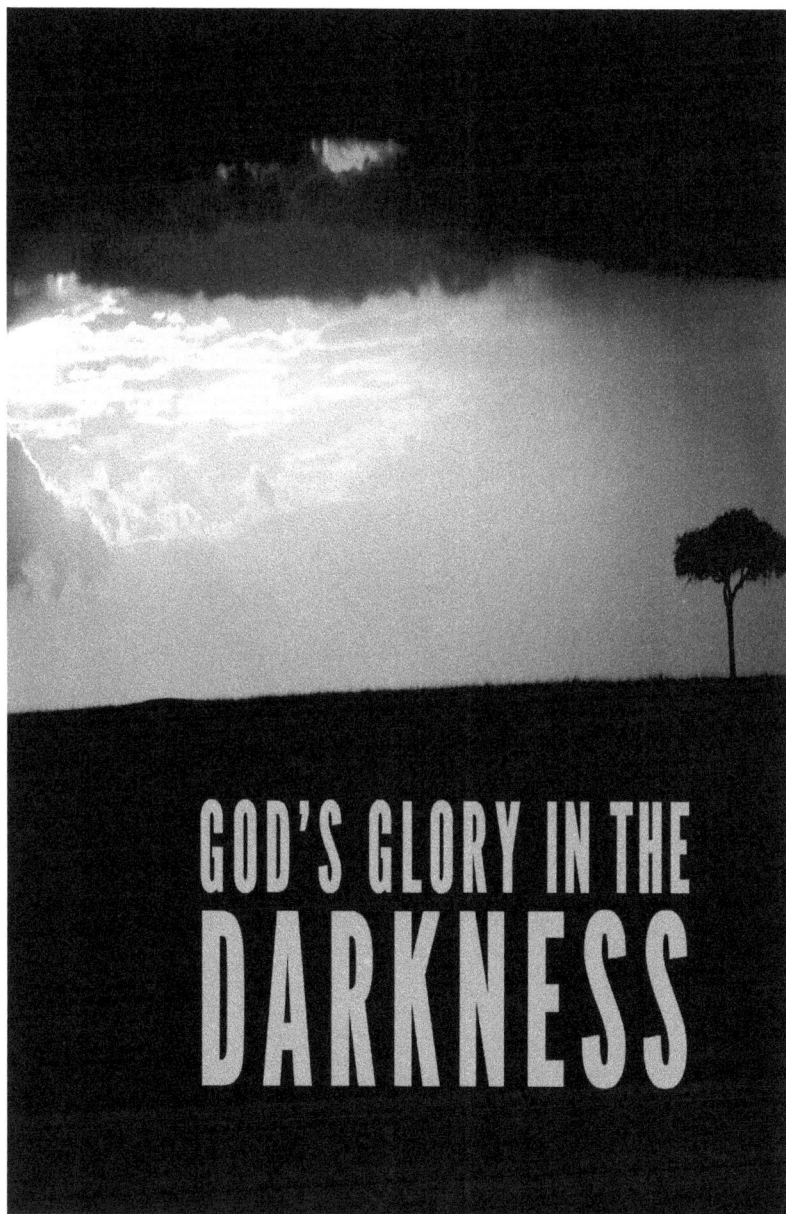

GOD'S GLORY IN THE
DARKNESS

Chapter 9
The Necessity of Light

Spiritual awakening in the Western world is not an option. It's a necessity.

We have entered a new era of world history, one in which darkness has the ability to spread more rapidly than previous generations could have ever imagined. As 2014 came to a close, reports of the expanding darkness were featured in the mainstream media in the United States. One of the most disturbing features of this darkness is the potential of global darkness merging with domestic forces of evil.

A gun-running ring was disrupted just before Christmas, 2014. The alarming part of the arrests was that the ring worked in and through airports in the United States. An employee of a major U.S. airline used his security clearance to smuggle guns through the Atlanta airport. He met a co-conspirator in the restroom inside the airport and gave him the guns. The co-conspirator then traveled to New York City and sold the guns. The illegal weapons were transported on at least twenty different flights.

After arresting the suspects, the Brooklyn District Attorney, Kenneth Thompson, described to reporters his grave concern about the incident. "If they can put guns on the plane this time, they could have easily put a bomb on one of those planes" (http://www.cnn.com/2014/12/23/us/delta-employee-gun-smuggling/). His concern was not only for the awful acts of violence created in New York by the smuggling ring, but also the potential for terrorists to find sympathetic persons and use them to unleash havoc upon the nation.

International transportation has produced a new urgency to the terrorist threat. A broker of darkness can be in a desert in the Middle East. Then, the same person can be in the heartland of the United States within a few hours. If the security systems of our major airports and transportation centers are breached, it leaves us vulnerable to darkness that we've never known.

We must not forget that groups like ISIS and Al Qaeda have the Western world in their sights. In the past, such groups have posed a threat to far away places, but with today's transportation and communication, we face a present danger far more vicious and ugly than anything we've ever known.

Islamic terrorists slaughtered 12 people at a satirical magazine office in Paris in January, 2015. One of the suspects had previously spent 18 months in jail for attempting to travel to Iraq to fight in a terrorist cell. The Islamists brought their barbaric acts to the West. Those deadly deeds appear to be a foreshadowing of things to come.

On December 22, 2014, Newsweek released a story about a German who was the first Western journalist embedded with ISIS. Jürgen Todenhöfer was given unparalleled access to ISIS for ten days. He shared some thoughts with CNN. "They are only 1% in the Islamic world, but this 1% movement has the power of a nuclear tsunami." He reported that he had met several Americans and a number of Europeans in ISIS. He told the German press there was a constant stream of men signing up to fight. "When we stayed at their recruitment house, there were 50 new fighters who came every day. And I just could not believe the glow in their eyes. They felt like they were coming to a promised land, like they were fighting for the right thing."

One fighter told Todenhöfer, "I would say that slavery is a great help to us and we will continue to have slavery and beheadings, it is part of our religion… many slaves have converted to Islam and have then been freed." The fighter then issued a warning to the West. "We will conquer Europe one day. It is not a question of if we will conquer Europe, just a matter of when that will happen. Our expansion will be perpetual… And the Europeans need to know that when we come, it will not be in a nice way. It will be with our weapons. And those who do not convert to Islam or pay the Islamic tax will be killed" (http://www.newsweek.com/german-journalist-returns-time-isis-chilling-stories-293781).

Can ISIS do what they threaten? I don't know if they have the capability. However, they do have the resolve and the emotional hatred to do incredible damage. Because of the ease of international transportation and the development of instant communication, we must take this darkness very seriously. Even if they are defeated in the Middle East, they have already infected followers from around the world with their vitriolic hatred. Solo attackers are already bringing their savagery to the streets of Western Europe and the United States.

How then should Christians in the West respond to the rapidly growing darkness? I'm convinced we must be filled with an equal amount but different kind of emotion and resolve. We must determine to seek God for a mighty spiritual awakening, perhaps one greater than any we have ever known. We must be filled with the love of God. Our expansion must be rooted in Christ-like character and a love for people. We must share our faith with a new sense of urgency and courage. And, above all, we must seek God for revival and depend upon Him completely.

Darkness often becomes so expansive that it drives Christians to seek God. Dark circumstances increase to such an extent that we are finally awakened to our need for God. When we become committed to seek God for a mighty revival, we are on the way to see the light shatter the darkness. It may take an extended period of time before the light bursts into the hearts of people, but it will definitely take place. I observed this in East Germany and Romania.

Pastor Liviu Olah called for people to pray in the mid-1970s, but it wasn't until December, 1989 that the light of God's glory erupted in Romania. The people prayed, yet the darkness continued to grow. I often thought that it would be impossible for the situation to get worse for followers of Jesus. But the darkness grew. Then, in one divine moment, light flooded the hearts of the population and changed the course of the nation.

There was a critical turning point that also took place in East Germany. I related the story of Pastor Busch in *Character in the Darkness*. When East Germany was at a very dark hour, he refused to relinquish his hope. He wasn't the only person in the country who sought God for a great outpouring of His Spirit. At about the same time, Pastor Busch encouraged me to attend the Communist Youth World Festival, a pastor in a small village in East Germany attempted to minister to the youth of his community. However, there was very little interest. The small village pastor and a friend decided to spend a year in prayer. They met weekly to seek God for a spiritual awakening among the youth. They heard about *The Jesus Movement* in the United States and prayed that God would work in a similar manner among their young people.

After a year of praying weekly, they took fourteen days for intensive prayer and fasting. The two men then started a meeting for young people with about 60 youth attending. It grew to 100, then 200. They kept praying and ministering to the young people. It continued to grow to 500 and later 1,000. Young people from throughout East Germany attended. They camped out for the weekend in the village and listened to the pastor teach the Bible.

The meetings grew so large that they decided to start conducting them in five major urban centers. I met some of the young people involved in those gatherings when I infiltrated the Communist Youth Fest to share Jesus. They invited me to visit their cities. I was deeply moved when I traveled to Dresden and Leipzig. Thousands of youth filled huge cathedrals and worshipped Jesus. When I went to the meeting in Dresden, I had to wait outside the church for the first group to conclude their worship. The cathedral was packed with about 2,000 youth. When they filed out, another 2,000 poured into the church. As I walked into the building with my East German friends, I remembered the first time I had visited a church in East Berlin with Pastor Busch. No young people were to be found anywhere. As the movement spread from a small village to the urban centers, churches couldn't contain the youth! Everything had turned around when one pastor in a rural community prayed and sought God.

It doesn't take a gifted communicator to transform a nation and repel the darkness. It only takes a humble, praying man or woman. The tide of darkness can be turned back. The evil forces of ISIS may have the emotional power of a tsunami as the German journalist indicated. However, they don't have the spiritual force of heaven as God's word clearly proclaims.

The East German pastor had an understanding of the nature of the darkness in his generation. But, more important, he understood the power of the light of the gospel and the tremendous potency of prayer.

My concern is that groups like ISIS have a commitment to darkness that is much greater than the commitment to the light that Christians carry. Darkness cannot remain when light enters the room. We who carry the light must resolve to turn our hearts toward heaven and seek God as we've never sought Him. Revival is not an alternative to darkness. It's essential to Western civilization. The times in which we live demand a mighty outpouring of His Spirit.

Micah Halpern, a journalist and analyst in the areas of terror, the Middle East, and Muslim Fundamentalism, wrote an eye-opening article in *The New York Observer*. He wrote, "The problem does not lie with the West's assessment of ISIS' military strength. The problem lies with the West's understanding of ISIS' expansive vision.

"The West does not see the big picture, even though ISIS is painting it for us. The conquest of Iraq and Syria and of a few other countries in the Levant is a big deal as far as the West is concerned, but it pales in comparison to ISIS' true objective, which is no less than conquering the entire world and to converting it into an Islamic society. The West has yet to comprehend that" (http://observer.com/2014/12/isis-intends-to-conquer-the-entire-world-and-create-an-islamic-society/).

I'm convinced we must awaken. We must seek God for revival. It's imperative. After I wrote the first section in this book, *The Approaching Darkness*, one of the respected Christian leaders in Pakistan responded to what I shared about his country. He wrote, "Right now there is a great need for men and women of God to stand in the gap and pray for the nation of Pakistan, especially the

Christian community. God is looking for watchmen who would stand on the walls for Pakistan.

"This is the time for us as Christian leaders to apply 2 Chronicles 7:14 to ourselves. It's the time to remove denominational barriers and be one in Christ Jesus. We must not give opportunities for hatred, disunity and divisions in our lives. We know we need to be one, but let us do it practically. Hard days are coming. I am not discouraged, but the incident in Peshawar was just a trailer for the actual movie. Stand with us and pray." (Note: Peshawar is the incident of which I wrote in *The Approaching Darkness* when 100 Christians were brutally murdered by terrorists.)

My friend in Pakistan has lived in the neighborhood of darkness. He knows its destructive path. He understands its ultimate goals. I don't write about these incidents to be an alarmist. But those of us who have walked into or lived in such dark places grasp the horror of the approaching darkness. This is no far away nightmare for my Pakistani friend. It's today's reality. There are a few journalists like Micah Halpern who have issued warnings about a coming darkness. It's time for the Christian community to awaken. Yes, we must wake up! In simple but clear terms, we desperately need a revival in this generation. We need a spiritual awakening that will transform our culture and repel the darkness. We need God's presence among us. Revival is not optional. It's absolutely necessary.

౭౩

Revival in the Family

Spiritual Awakening is not only necessary because of the looming international threat, but also because of the collapse of the family. Forces of darkness have been successful in redefining the family in the Western world. At first, divorce soared and couples living together became the norm for society. Then, political and cultural pressure redefined the family unit. They proclaimed that the nature of a family didn't have to consist of a man and a woman in a committed relationship for life.

Western culture slowly but surely bought into the redefinition of the family. The cultural shift was so strong that those who held to the Biblical view of the family have often been viewed as bigots. Concern has grown in many Christian circles about a heavy-handedness applied to church leaders who disagree with the newly espoused definition of the family.

When God created man, the first institution He established was the family. The Bible clearly states, "Therefore a man shall leave his father and his mother and hold fast to his wife, and they shall become one flesh" (Genesis 2:24). It was in the context of this commandment that life would be birthed. God established that a man and woman would live together in the most intimate of human relationships and children would be born in such relationships. When this institution collapses, it opens the door for global darkness as well as personal darkness to spread rapidly.

It's not just that we need Biblically-defined family units, but we must have healthy relationships within our homes. I'm convinced there never would have been an emergence of an alternative definition of the family if our relationships had been in good shape. The destruction of solid family ties opened doors to wreck healthy homes.

We can't point our fingers and blame those who disagree with us. We desperately need God to search our own hearts. We've often accepted a distorted image of a healthy home by comparing ourselves to others. We live in a culture where it's easy to think, *I have a strong and healthy family compared to others.*

I struggled with that attitude around the time I first visited Romania. I traveled to the country in 1980 and saw things I had only read in history books. God was moving in the churches in a remarkable manner. Pastor's Liviu's teachings on prayer and repentance had taken hold of the people and the fruit could easily be seen. Churches were packed everywhere that I traveled—— not because I visited them. No one knew I was coming. In spite of severe persecution, it was their normal attendance. People stood outside the buildings to listen. They stood down the aisles and around the platform. It was remarkable to see light shining at such a dark moment.

When I came home from that first trip to Romania, my wife Tex and I made plans to return. I had witnessed God's glory in one of the darkest places in the world, and I wanted her to experience this historic movement of God's Spirit. However, there was a work that God needed to accomplish in our hearts before He allowed us to go back.

As we prepared for our next visit to Romania, our son became ill. There seemed to be no solution to his sickness. We prayed. We sought the best medical treatment possible, but nothing worked. When I returned from my office one afternoon, tears were running down the cheeks of my wife. "Sammy, I need to talk to you."

Those words took us on a journey upon which we experienced a great renewal in our relationship. I took several days off from the church where I was pastor, and Tex and I spent time seeking God. He applied His healing oil to our relationship and sent revival to our home. I'm convinced we were headed down a path that would have led to the destruction of our home if we hadn't experienced this deep work of God in our hearts. God showed me my arrogance and how it had hurt my wife. He opened her eyes to see her bitterness that affected our communication with one another.

We were broken before God. It was then that He healed our hurting hearts and ultimately healed our son. He restored our relationship, and we rebuilt our home. If someone would have asked me before that experience if we had a healthy home, I would have answered, "Of course we do. Our relationship is far better than most families." That would have been a true statement. However, in this generation it's not difficult to have a good husband/wife relationship *compared to others*.

Revival in our family enabled us to return to Romania with a relevant message burning deep within our souls. I'm convinced that the deep work of God in my wife and myself kept us from shipwreck. That renewal in our lives transpired 25 years ago, nearly a decade before the Romanian Revolution. If we had not experienced such a revival, we would have missed one of the greatest spiritual awakenings in the last century, the revolution in Romania.

இ

God's Glory in the Church

As I've looked back upon the movement of God's Spirit that transformed East Germany and Romania, I've asked myself what we can learn from those outpourings of God's Spirit. The first thing I learned from those believers was their unbroken commitment and resolve to pray for and work towards revival. They didn't pray for a few days or weeks. They prayed for years. In the case of Pastor Liviu Olah, he was deported from Romania long before freedom came to the nation. It was about 15 years from the time he initially called the people to pray until the day when God transformed the country.

We often pray for a few weeks. Christians in the West are great in launching a new program of prayer or initiating a new emphasis on renewal. However, I don't think we've understood that revival is not a fast food item on the Bible's menu. There's no shortcut to spiritual awakening. It will come in God's time if we persist in seeking Him.

God longs to display His glory in His church. He loves the church. He sent Jesus to die for the church. When we humble ourselves, pray and seek God's face, and turn from our sins, we position ourselves to see God's glory displayed. The glory of God is the greatest reason we desperately need a spiritual awakening. A deep work of God will restore a broken culture and renew our most important relationships. Those are great reasons to seek God for revival.

However, there's one motivation for seeking God for a great revival that's far greater than those already mentioned. It's not centered in our needs, but in His worthiness. The focus of this rationale isn't our weaknesses, but His power. It's not rooted in our hurts, but in His grace. It's not to enable the growth of our churches, but to release the coming of His kingdom. It's not to build our reputations, but to bestow upon Him glory, honor, and praise. That's why we need revival! Our goal must be much greater than the defeat of the global and domestic darkness. Our objective must point to a glorious display of the One who is light. We need to see His beauty and splendor. We must fix our aim upon the glory of God. That must become the one great reason we long for revival.

Chapter 10
Penetrating the Darkness

If our passion is for the glory of God, then we must not sit on the sidelines as cheerleaders. God's love compels us to carry the light into the darkness. I've witnessed light shatter darkness on numerous occasions in various parts of the world. I've never seen a spiritual awakening take place when the light retreated to a "safe place."

The "safe place" is not as secure as many think. Retreating to the safety of shadows only delays the arrival of darkness. It will still cover our communities, perhaps slowly, but surely. Darkness can be scary because of the unknown dwelling inside it. We must understand that darkness can roar like a lion, but it can't destroy those carrying the light. We must never retreat, but be filled with love and humility, bringing light into the deepest parts of the darkness.

It was a frightening feeling in the early 1970s when Pastor Busch challenged me to infiltrate the Communist Youth World Festival in East Berlin and share the love of Jesus with 100,000 atheistic youth. My first reaction was one of retreat— to say no and go back to the safety of the West. However, God's Spirit spoke quietly to my heart, and East Berlin beckoned. I returned to my home and asked two friends to pray with me about returning to East Berlin to share the gospel.

Fred Starkweather and Fred Bishop felt they should be a part of the outreach. We knew the starting place for this impossible task was prayer and decided to take a day of prayer and fasting. As we sought God that day, we had a clear impression that we would be able to publicly share the gospel. That seemed ludicrous. Christians were persecuted in East Germany, and we wondered how it would be possible to speak publicly about Jesus.

However, as we prayed and fasted, God reminded us of a passage about fasting. In Isaiah 58:6, a question is asked, "Is not this the fast that I choose?" The next two verses contained a very interesting response. "Is it not to share your bread with the hungry…? Then shall your light break forth like the dawn, and your healing shall spring up speedily; your righteousness shall go before you; the glory of the Lord shall be your rear guard."

As we read the Scriptures, we were convinced that God would allow us to share the bread of life with hungry communist youth. But, the last part of the verse blew our minds: "the glory of the Lord shall be your rear guard." I wondered if it were remotely possible that we would see the glory of the Lord. Yet, that was what the verse indicated. Five of us made our way to Berlin: My wife, Tex, me, and our two-year old son, Dave, along with Fred Bishop and Fred Starkweather.

Once we arrived, we all stayed in a Lutheran retreat center in West Berlin. Tex and Dave remained in West Berlin while Fred Bishop, Fred Starkweather, and I traveled daily to East Berlin. Before we left for the East, we spent time in prayer during the mornings, fervently seeking God. We were simply three foolish young men who only wanted to trust God and share His light with communist young people. We were way over our heads and we knew it, but we remembered Pastor Busch's exhortation, "With men it is impossible, but with God nothing is impossible."

Our first test of facing the impossible came at the border crossing. We had stuffed our clothes with Christian pamphlets that explained the love of God. Every fourth or fifth person was pulled from the line, taken to a back room, and searched thoroughly. We silently prayed, "Lord, we're trusting you to get us across." He did. The eyes of the border guard crossed over us as he picked people before and behind us. We experienced something similar throughout the entire festival.

When we arrived in Alexanderplatz, the place where many of the youth congregated, we found the plaza packed with *Free German Youth,* all wearing blue shirts. It was like a sea of communist youth filling the large open area. Soldiers and police were everywhere. My heart sank, and I doubted the promise God had given us. As far as the eye could see to the north, south, east, and west, there was nothing but young people, policemen, and soldiers.

My heart just ripped apart for these young people. My eyes bulged as I tried to take it all in. Silently we prayed, "Lord, there are just three of us. How can we reach these kids? How can we do it?"

As we walked through the crowds, my heart broke. Then my eyes caught something unbelievable. One of the communist youth had a small sticker on his shirt that read, "One way, Jesus!"

I wondered, *Could this be a Christian, communist young person?* I approached him and asked in German about his sticker. He said he found it on the ground. I then asked him if he understood the meaning, and he replied negatively. I shared about Jesus. He told me he had been taught all his life that there was no God. He continued, "This is very interesting. I want to hear more."

As I talked with the young man, I noticed a crowd gathering around us. People were listening intently to our conversation. I guessed they could tell I was not German because of my poor grammar and American accent. I felt embarrassed about my poor German until the crowd pressed in and asked if we were Americans. Everyone wanted autographs of Americans!

The Lord gave us an idea as the kids asked us to sign their kerchiefs. Fred Starkweather wrote in German, "God loves you and has a wonderful plan for your life" and then signed his name. Fred Bishop wrote, "But man is sinful and separated from a holy God" and signed his name. I then wrote, "Jesus is God's provision for our sins. Trust Him and find forgiveness" and signed my name. We must have signed three hundred scarves that evening.

I felt the presence of God upon us and I became more and more bold as we shared Christ with various kids. I couldn't forget the promise that the glory of God would be our rear guard. I knew the time had come. I grabbed Fred Bishop and Fred Starkweather and told them I was going to do more than share one on one. I was going to preach.

I began speaking loudly and hundreds of young people gathered around me. Hundreds of hungry hearts listened attentively as we shared the gospel. When we returned to West Berlin, it was difficult to go to sleep that night. I shared with Tex all that had transpired. God answered our prayers, and it was only the first day.

When we returned to Alexanderplatz the next day, the place was filled with young people. But everything was much quieter than the first day. As we walked around the plaza, I felt we needed to find a place to pray. However, Fred Bishop said, "I think we need to do it right here."

I glanced at several communist soldiers standing nearby and said, "I don't think so."

Fred insisted, and we knelt in a small huddle and prayed. As I came to the end of my prayer, I said, "In Jesus name, amen." I knew a crowd had gathered, but I hardly noticed it as I rose. The Spirit of God came upon me with such fullness that I was *lifted* from my knees. Before I was fully erect, I began preaching the gospel and continued for four hours. That was truly a miracle, because I didn't know four hours of German! There have only been a few times in my ministry that I have felt the anointing of God as much as that moment.

Suddenly, I noticed the Communist soldiers breaking through the crowd. I thought of Tex and Dave, of Siberian prison camps and losing a decade of my precious freedom. As the soldiers reached me, I hesitated, waiting for those fateful words, "You're under arrest."

They never came. Instead, they began firing one question after another.

"Who is Jesus?"

"How do you know He's real?"

It was incredible. The crowd picked up on the questions, asking the same things, talking at once.

An atheist called for silence. "I don't believe in God," he said, but this man has something to say and we must listen. The crowd is too large for those in the back to hear. Let's spread out and sit down."

I sat and fielded questions, preaching to this multitude and being full of the joy of the Lord. A love for them welled up within me and I felt an immense assurance that now, as never before, I was in the exact center of the perfect will of God. I once again spoke and answered questions for several hours. As the crowd finally broke up, a girl with long brown hair walked by and said in a confidential tone, "I cannot talk to you now. If I'm seen, I will be in very much trouble. Can I meet you tomorrow?"

"Yes," I said. "At the fountain late tomorrow afternoon at 6:30."

When we arrived back in West Berlin, I told Tex about our experience. I shared with her about the soldiers, the atheist, and all the questions. I told her about the mysterious girl. As we all discussed it, we felt we had made contact with a secret believer that we had read so much about.

When we returned to East Berlin on the third day, we found people walking around looking for *The Jesus People*. Kids came up to us asking if we were going to be preaching that night. We assured them that we would.

Finally, Ilse, the girl with dark brown hair, showed up. She brought her brother and another girl. They were a part of the Christian meetings that the East German from the rural town had started. They had been praying, and God directed them to go the Communist Youth World Festival. They felt they would meet some Christians there. An atheist meeting isn't exactly the place you'd look for other Christians, but they did! We talked with them briefly before people gathered around us again.

The connection with *Ilse* and her friends began a relationship with underground believers that lasted until the collapse of Communism. I don't have time in this chapter to relate all that God did during the Communist Youth World Festival. We hope to release the full story in 2016. Suffice it to say that we saw the glory of God within the next several days. We even held a *Jesus March* one night!

As the week progressed, the authorities attempted to break up one of our meetings. They were trying to impress the youth with their "freedom," and that's why they never arrested us. They used other tactics. They trained groups of young people to break up our meetings. After they broke up the meeting one particular night, several of the new believers said to me, "Let's don't stop. Let's make an impression on the entire festival."

I said, "Okay. Follow me." We created a small group marching, singing, and playing guitars. Young people saw us and thought it was an official game. Hundreds followed behind us. I preached to thousands of Communist youth that night. God blessed and the glory of the Lord filled Alexanderplatz. From the Communist Youth World Festival, our ministry was launched to the communist world for sixteen years— until the Berlin Wall came down and Communism collapsed.

As the communist empire collapsed in the late 1989s and early 1990s, God opened doors to preach in stadiums throughout Eastern Europe and the former Soviet Union. I was even able to preach in the stadiums of the cities of the Siberian prison camps. But it all began at Alexanderplatz in East Berlin in the middle of darkness.

❦

Three Truths Learned

I learned several great lessons from my experience at the Communist Youth World Festival. *The glory of the Lord is manifested when we take the light of the gospel into the darkness.* If we want to see God's glory shining brightly, we can't remain in our comfort zones. Too many of us have settled for attainable goals. We've become satisfied with wanting to see the reflection of the moon at night rather than beholding the radiance of the glory of the Son! We need a reset of purpose and priorities. We've aimed too low in life. We must re-evaluate our goals during these dark days. We need more for our nation than just to dispel the darkness. We need more than church growth. We need more than healthier homes. We need the glory of God in our midst.

Second, we need a baptism of love from above. When I went to the Communist Youth World Festival, the communists were the enemy. Very few people thought about reaching them with the gospel. Most people only saw them as evil. However, when I walked through the crowds in Alexanderplatz, God's love poured from heaven upon my soul. I saw those young people as human beings created in God's image. I saw a spiritual battle that was taking place for their hearts. I saw them through the eyes of Jesus. He loved them. He died for them. The wonderful passage of Scripture, "For God so loved the world…." (John 3:16) applied to them as much as it did me.

When God's love floods our souls, we will change the course of history. I only experienced God's love as I walked among those young people. I went to East Berlin out of obedience to God, but left with His love filling my heart. It's difficult for love to be manifested in isolation. Love requires that we step into the lives of others and minister to them. God will move heaven to Earth when we take such a step because that's the way He loves. God didn't sit in heaven, shouting down to Earth, "I love you! I love you!" No, He took upon Himself human flesh. He came to this planet and loved as no one has ever loved. He lived as no one has ever lived. He was called Immanuel, which means God with us.

Finally, we must make prayer a priority if we are to see the glory of God. What happened in East Berlin was birthed in the hearts of two East German pastors: one in East Berlin and the other in a small mountain village. Both prayed for God to move among the youth of the nation. When we met Pastor Busch, he somehow knew that meeting was an answer to his prayer. The interesting thing is that his idea was so impossible that I couldn't attempt it without making prayer a priority. His prayer set me to seeking God, and that brought another group of people into the network of intercessors.

Prayer births prayer. We must understand that we can do church work in our own power. We can build strategies with our cleverness. We can influence people with our speech and writing. But, we can only see God's glory through prayer.

Many years ago, I asked God to put me in a position where I could not do His work *in my power*. When Pastor Busch challenged me to go to the World Festival, I knew I couldn't do what he was asking. I knew it would call for God's power to accomplish His will. Each of us must ask if we have been doing God's work in our own power or in the power of the Holy Spirit. It's only when we're in the place of absolute dependence upon Him that we will see much more than good works. In the place of prayer we will see the glory of God.

❧

What to Expect

When we place ourselves at God's disposal and break out of our comfort zones, we need to know what to anticipate. There is a cost to following Jesus. Many desire to experience a type of Pentecost— but without the *cost*. God doesn't go around showing His glory in a flippant manner. He longs to show us His glory, but we must be willing to seek Him with our entire hearts.

I believe three things will transpire when we penetrate the darkness. *We will see people come to Christ.* As I've walked into dark areas of the world, I've found one common denominator: hungry hearts. It doesn't matter whether it has been in a secular, atheistic environment like East Berlin or in a war zone like Burundi. It doesn't even matter if the circumstances have been in very religious environments like Iran. People are the same. There's a God-shaped vacuum that religion, education, and power cannot fill. They leave the human heart empty. It's only when Jesus dwells in the human heart that the darkness is dispelled. Once we enter the dark areas of our culture, we'll find hungry hearts, and people will come to Christ.

I wish I could say that everyone will come to Christ, but that's not true, or even close to being realistic. *Some people will reject our message, and a few may even hate us.* It would be wrong for me to tell you that when you penetrate the darkness, everything will be calm, and you'll win a popularity contest. It doesn't happen that way. We faced difficulties at the communist festival and were opposed by the brokers of darkness. However, the opposition was pale compared to the glory of God we experienced.

In the gospel of John chapter fifteen, Jesus told His disciples that if people hated Him, then they would also hate those who follow Him. Immediately before He spoke those words, He spoke of the great commandment— loving others. A person who determines to penetrate the darkness must likewise determine to love those who hate him.

When a Christian decides to penetrate the darkness, that person has the potential of seeing God's glory. If I learned anything during the Communist Youth World Festival, I came to understand that God's heart longs to bring those living in darkness into His wonderful light. When our attitudes and actions line up with the heart of God, He will release all heaven to bring about His will.

God loves people. That's a simple but profound statement. I don't think that most of us understand how great His love is. It's in the display of His love that we see His glory. When His love fills our hearts, we will be thrust into a dark world with the light of the gospel. The glory of His light is manifested when the rays of His love shine during the dark nights. When we penetrate the darkness we see the radiance of His glory and the splendor of His love. And that is— revival.

Chapter 11
Discipleship in the Darkness

Not only does prayer birth more prayer, but faith produces more faith. After the genocide in Rwanda, I was asked to conduct an evangelistic meeting as well as work with leaders in the devastated nation. God worked in such a marvelous manner that faith brought more faith in the heart of Pastor Joseph Karasanyi. He sent a fax to our office, stating that he believed all of Africa needed our message. The fax included a map of the continent, and Joseph had written numbers in the center of each country. Each number represented the priority and urgency of going to that nation. He asked me to study the map and then call him to discuss it.

As I examined the map, I noticed that he had listed a number of war-torn countries as high priorities. He had also categorized a predominantly Islamic nation as a major concern. When I spoke with him about the map, I asked if he knew anyone in the Islamic nation. (For security reasons, I'll not mention the name of the country.) He assured me that he had contacts. I still had questions because I knew this nation was overwhelmingly Muslim. I questioned whether it was possible to conduct a large evangelistic meeting there. However, his faith had grown rapidly, and he felt certain that we could.

My colleague, Mike Scalf, met Joseph in the country. Mike laughed when he learned that Joseph did have a contact there. When Mike told me about it, he emphasized the word "**a**" as in one. Yet, Mike and Joseph knew how to proceed with their investigation: **pray.** God led them to a group of pastors and leaders with a heart to reach their people with the gospel. Joseph shared how God had worked in Rwanda, and Mike spoke about our ministry.

One of the pastors listened intently and after a few moments asked, "What did you say the evangelist's name is?" Mike gave my name. The pastor left immediately and came back with a copy of my book, *The Prayer Factor.* "Is this the same man?"

Mike grinned. "Yes."

The leaders invited me to the country not long afterward. When I went there, it was one of the greatest spiritual harvests of my ministry. Thousands of people came to Christ. The most impressive thing that took place was not the harvest, but how the believers in this nation helped the new believers grow in their faith. Every person who came to Christ was integrated into a small group Bible study within seventy-two hours of their commitment to Jesus. The new followers of Jesus immediately learned the basics of Christian living.

At that time, none us knew what would transpire in the Middle East in the next few years. The *Arab Spring* had turned into the *Arab Nightmare* as fundamentalist Muslims took control of large amounts of territory throughout the Middle East. God had shown His glory and had prepared believers in this nation for a harvest before radical Islam would take control of the area. Much of the preparation for this work of God came because Christians had prepared for an outpouring of God's Spirit through small group discipleship.

I've noticed the same strategy has been incorporated in several nations where I've seen God's light shatter darkness. I'm also aware that many Christians in the West have been praying for a great spiritual awakening. People have asked me, "Why haven't we seen God answer our prayers?"

I don't have the full answer to that question. However, God knows our hearts and our needs. I'm sure He will answer our prayers in His time and way. But there are other questions that must be asked. "Why would God send a great awakening when we aren't prepared or we don't do anything to get ready for it? Why would He send a revival to a church if people went out the back door as fast as they came in the front? Why would He allow spiritual children to be birthed if we haven't made provisions to care for them?"

If we long to see God's glory, then we need a repository to house the outpouring of His Spirit. God has given us this kind of container. We can clearly see it through the life of Jesus. He called a small group of men and women to follow Him. He then spent time with them, taught them, and lived out His teachings in their presence.

തs

Characteristics of Discipleship

There were three characteristics of the training that Jesus gave His disciples. First, *He was very clear about the cost of following Him.* Second, *He taught eternal truths about God, life, and relationships.* Third, *He demonstrated how to live those truths by the manner in which He lived.*

There's much talk among Christians in our generation about making disciples of Jesus, but little discussion about the cost of discipleship. When we leave the price of following Jesus out of our discussion, we carve a hole in the vessel that God has given to contain the movement of God's Spirit. Jesus told those wanting to follow Him, "If anyone would come after me, let him deny himself and take up his cross daily and follow me. For whoever would save his life will lose it, but whoever loses his life for my sake will save it" (Luke 9:23, 24 ESV). He was very clear about the cost of following Him.

When we commit ourselves to penetrating the darkness, it will require that we count the cost of following Jesus.

In the previous section in this book, *Character in the Darkness*, I told the story of a great movement of God's Spirit in war-torn Burundi. Mike Scalf and Joseph Karasanyi, who had travelled to the Middle East, went to Burundi at great risk to their lives. Mike and I had prayed and felt he and Joseph should go into the country ahead of me to assist the local leaders with preparations. We had a sense that God would work in a wonderful way.

As Mike reviewed his documents on the way to Burundi, he read a U.S. State Department warning. *The Department of State warns U.S. citizens of the risks of traveling to Burundi, urges U.S. citizens to avoid all travel and advises you to consider carefully the risks of travel.* Mike had to count the cost of making known the love of God in this dark war zone. He did. And it cost him greatly.

Major Pierre Buyoya had come into power through a military coup, and neighboring countries had slapped sanctions on the nation. That made entry into Burundi very difficult for Mike. He met Joseph in Rwanda where he was able to secure a visa. Because of the sanctions, the international airport in Bujumbura, the capital, was closed, and flights weren't allowed into the country.

However, Mike and Joseph hired a pilot from a small air cargo company in Rwanda to fly them into Bujumbura.

The pilot was so fearful of the trip that he landed, kept the plane on an outer end of the tarmac, and told Joseph and Mike to get off the plane. "This stop hasn't been filed with anyone. No one knows we're here. You must leave quickly." The two men took a deep breath and got off the plane. No one was waiting for them, and the airport looked like a ghost town. It was a long, lonely walk to the bullet-riddled terminal. Joseph used his cell phone to call one of the pastors, and he came immediately to pick them up.

Mike stayed at a somewhat empty European-style hotel, while Joseph lodged nearby. After the first night of meeting with the pastors, Joseph returned to his quarters. As he arrived, three men stepped out of a dark area and grabbed him. They demanded three thousand dollars. "We know who you are and who you're working with. You must tell your American friends to come up with the money. We will return when your American evangelist friend arrives."

The threat to Joseph was only one of many difficulties that were thrust on the two of them. Mike became very ill and started running a high fever. Even though Mike's wife Norma didn't know about his sickness, she made an emergency call into Burundi. She needed to let Mike know that his mother had become critically ill and had to be brought to the hospital.

As soon as Norma spoke with Mike, she became extremely concerned and knew his condition was serious. Meanwhile, I had just completed preaching in Scotland, and my wife and I were in a London hotel. We were preparing to fly to Rwanda the next day and on to Burundi with the same cargo company that had transported Mike and Joseph. Norma called us while we were in London.

"Sammy, I just talked to Mike. He's extremely ill. He's running a fever and having hallucinations, and I'm scared to death for him. And that's not all. His mother has been taken to the hospital, and they don't think she's going to live more than a couple of days." She then told me about the threats against Joseph and the money that had been demanded.

"Norma, I need to talk to Mike immediately. If he's that sick, we need to get him out of the country."

When I finished talking with Norma, Tex and I pleaded with God for guidance. I then called Mike, and he sounded awful. I told him, "We need to get you out of there."

"Sammy," he said, "There's no way out of here. This place is about to explode."

I immediately called pastor friends in the United States and asked them and their churches to pray for Mike and the situation in Burundi. I stayed up all night crying out to God and sending emails to friends asking them to pray. I called Mike again the next day. "Mike, you need to have Joseph stay with you in your hotel. We have to find a way for you to get out of the country."

Joseph went to the lobby and experienced a miracle. A pilot was at the hotel desk. He had privately flown a person into the country and was about to leave. Joseph made arrangements for Mike to be on the flight with him. Mike made it safely to Uganda and received medical treatment.

When Mike landed in the United States, he received a call from our pastor. Mike's mother had passed.

As I shared with you about Burundi in *Character in the Darkness*, we saw God move mightily in this war-torn country. God worked so marvelously that the head of peace negotiations asked us to take the gospel message to everyone in Burundi. God's glory filled the stadium as warring groups came together.

However, this work of God's Spirit came with a price for Mike Scalf. He risked everything for the sake of the gospel. He suffered. But God used him to prepare the way for light to shatter darkness.

Most of us won't go through the suffering that Mike experienced, but we must understand that there's a cost to following Jesus. In the West, we often speak of the benefits of following Jesus, but seldom of the cost. There's been a common denominator in every place that I've seen God's Spirit dispel darkness. Someone has been willing to pay a price to allow God to use him. This was not only true in Burundi, but also in Romania, Iran, East Germany, and numerous other countries. As we make disciples, we must tell those followers of Jesus what He told all of us. There's a cost involved in following Him if we want to penetrate the darkness.

❧

The Scriptures and Discipleship

The pursuit of discipleship is the quest for Christ-likeness. If our aim is to become like Him, we must then ask, *"How do we do that?"* The answer to that query isn't a secret. The Bible paints a clear picture of the character of Christ. It gives examples of His love and justice. It declares the truths about life that He embraced. It shows us His actions when He faced difficulties. He spent time with a small band of men and women teaching them these life principles.

Discipleship requires that we know the heart and lifestyle of Jesus. We can't live the kind of life He desires for us if we don't know what He aspires for us. One of the great needs today is to learn those Biblical truths that teach how to become like Jesus. The early followers of Jesus were called followers of *The Way* because they had followed the way of life that Jesus taught and lived.

As darkness grows, it attempts to exterminate the light of God's word. It fears the light and will do everything within its power to extinguish it. That is exactly what I saw had transpired the first time I arrived at the Romanian border during the days of the dictator, Nicolae Ceauşescu. A youth music group travelled with me in 1980 because our mission was to reach the young people of the nation with the message of Christ.

Border guards demanded that we get out of the van in which we were traveling. They searched it thoroughly and went through our luggage. Each of us had a personal Bible. They confiscated them and said that they would return the Bibles when we left Romania. That experience was the norm every time I travelled there. The first question asked by border guards was ordinarily, "Do you have any Bibles?" It became very dangerous to carry them. After a couple of trips into the country, I quit taking my Bible and started memorizing the Scriptures because I knew it was impossible for the border guards to see inside my heart. When I preached, I preached from memory.

Even though the government hated the light, I also found the opposite to be true. Christians had a deep respect and admiration for the Bible. They loved to hear Biblical teachings. When I preached from the Scriptures, it was as though I had opened a dam and the living water of God's Spirit flooded their thirsty hearts. Their longing to hear the Bible was quite remarkable. I had never seen anything like it anywhere in the world.

They didn't just love to hear the word of God, but they memorized it with such fervor that I had never seen. Three young Romanians made an incredible impact upon my life. Paul Negrut was a young psychologist when I first went to Romania. He was the first person to translate for me. Radu Gheorgita had just completed his military service and travelled with me throughout the country the first time I went there. Dr. Titus Cotea was a medical doctor with a heart to see the gospel spread throughout the nation. All three had one thing in common. They had all memorized an incredible amount of the Bible.

Titus travelled with me on many occasions. One day he shared with me a revolutionary idea. "Let's bring a singing group made up of Romanian youth to other parts of the country."

My eyes bulged. "You have to be kidding. That would be extremely dangerous for them."

Titus' eyes pierced mine. "I'm not kidding. They will have to be willing to pay the price. They may be arrested. I don't know what will happen. But if young people around the nation see other Romanian youth serving God, it will inspire a new generation to follow Jesus."

I reluctantly agreed. When I returned to the country, Titus had a select group of young people and trained them to sing and speak in the services. It took my breath away when I heard them. Their singing was decent, but their speaking was astonishing. They quoted the Scriptures— not just a verse or two. Each one of them had memorized the books of James, 1 Peter, and 1 John, and recited them during the services. People in the congregations wept as they boldly quoted entire books of the Bible.

Paul Negrut was also a man of the Scriptures. He had memorized much of the Bible. After the Revolution he became President of the Evangelical Alliance and also the Baptist Union. He became one of the foremost leaders in the country. Radu Gehorgita became a Greek professor at Midwestern Baptist Theological Seminary in the United States after the Revolution. Many years after the Revolution, a friend of mine attended an international worship service in Jerusalem while on a tour there. A man in the service quoted the entire book of 1 Timothy. My

American friend introduced himself to the man. The man quoting the Scriptures was Radu.

Those who love the light love the Bible and for good reason. The Psalmist said, "Your word is a lamp to my feet and a light to my path" (Psalms 119:105 ESV). Christians living during the dark days of Romania knew the Bible was the light to show them how to travel during a dark and dangerous night.

☙

Applying the Scriptures

Being a disciple of Jesus is much more than knowing the Scriptures. It is applying them to our lives. True discipleship is much more than learning and teaching others about the Christian life. It's taking what we learn about the life of Jesus and making a concrete decision to practice what He taught and how He lived. We then depend upon the Holy Spirit to enable us to live in the manner God desires.

There is a simple but profound difference between Christianity in the dark and difficult places and the kind of Christianity that I've seen in the Western world. Often, when I speak in the West, Christians fill their notebooks with teachings from the Bible. However, Christians in the hard places fill their hearts with the teachings. The difference: one loves to gain information while the other attempts to apply truth.

When Dr. Titus Coltea and I travelled throughout Romania during Ceauşescu's reign, we developed a simple strategy. We would go into a city and teach the people about prayer. When we returned to that city the following year and conducted an evangelistic event, the results were overwhelming. We witnessed multitudes of people coming to Christ in every place we had previously visited. After we taught the Christians in Romania how to pray, they did just that. They prayed for their family, friends, and colleagues. By the time we returned, people were prepared to hear the gospel.

Often, when I speak among Christians in the West, people come with their notebooks, iPads, and recording devices. Everyone wants some new piece of information. If we are going to shatter the darkness, it won't happen because we've gained more knowledge than the brokers of darkness. Our power doesn't lie in our familiarity with truth, but in our obedience to it. It's then that we shall see the glory of God. Discipleship is much more than gaining understanding. It's practicing the truth we've come to understand.

Chapter 12
The Glory of God

Mike Fechner lived a comfortable lifestyle. He had not only become a prosperous entrepreneur, but most people would say that he had achieved success in his spiritual life. Mike attended church regularly, tithed, and loved his wife and children. Yet, Mike felt something missing in his spiritual journey.

It was when Mike met an African American woman that God showed him what was lacking. Velma, a financially struggling single mother, lived a life of faith that Mike had never seen. Her prayer life astonished him, and her love for Jesus challenged him.

Mike, a millionaire businessman, began mentoring Velma's son, Ramon. She became like a sister to Mike, and Ramon like one of his own children. He realized that the racial, economic, and social divide between the wealthy and poor districts of Dallas could be bridged through Christ. In 1992, Ramon was shot and killed in a random drive-by shooting. Eight others were killed in the same neighborhood that evening. Ramon's death became a catalyst for Mike to start a ministry to bridge the gap between the two communities. Mike began H.I.S. Bridge Builders to meet to the educational, economic, health, and spiritual needs of this poor, urban area.

As Mike allowed God's light to shine in his heart, he became God's instrument to shatter the darkness in that inner city neighborhood. His vision grew rapidly and his organization expanded their outreach to other cities. He brought the vision of transforming urban centers to several nations around the world. At the age of 48, Mike was diagnosed with stage IV lung cancer, but he couldn't be deterred. He served God and poor communities as long as God gave him the ability.

H.I.S. Bridge Builders were preparing for their annual fundraiser in April, 2014. Mike had become critically ill and would not be able to attend. Mike's son brought a film crew to him a couple of days before the event. Mike didn't have long to live, and he wanted a chance to speak to the supporters of the ministry. However, Mike was extremely weak and had a difficult time communicating.

He knew that life was short and soon he would be in the presence of Jesus. What one thing did he want to say? It was difficult for him to utter anything. Finally, he was able to speak what was on his heart: one word, one passion. *"Awakening."* He passed from this life into eternity just a couple days later. When Mike's brother, Ruben, told me what Mike had said, God gripped my heart. In Mike's last days on Earth, he spoke the message that is so desperately needed at this critical moment of history: *"Awakening!"*

എ

Awakening and the Glory of God

God has placed several signposts on the path leading to great awakenings. These indicators have been around for centuries. **Signpost #1—** When the church loses its passion for Christ, darkness makes a quiet but subtle approach into the culture. **Signpost #2—** If the church doesn't awaken, darkness quickly covers society. A tipping point comes, and Christians lose respect in the population. Persecution often arises. **Signpost #3—** Someone or a small group of people becomes concerned and seeks God for revival. The Holy Spirit then descends, producing brokenness and repentance in the hearts of God's people. **Signpost #4—** God's love floods the hearts of Christians. They reach out to those trapped in darkness and minister to them. **Signpost #5—** The Holy Spirit brings light back into the culture. Churches, communities, and entire nations experience a great spiritual awakening.

There have been three major awakenings and several minor ones throughout American history. When God's Spirit visits His people, His glory is manifested. People see the beauty and splendor of Jesus. It's amazing how quickly things change when He comes.

People often ask me, "What's the most dramatic experience you have had when you've gone to the dark and difficult places?" That's difficult to answer because God has done so much in so many different places. However, there's one place where I've witnessed deep darkness in the most impossible situation. I watched the splendor and glory of God burst upon a nation. I'll never forget what I saw and experienced there.

☙

The Glory of God in Romania

I've shared with you about Pastor Liviu Olah. I never had the opportunity to meet him because he had been put out of the country by the time I initially entered Romania. I made my first trip into the country in June 1980. I continued travelling into the nation two to three times per year until August, 1988. I was then arrested and put out of the country and told I'd never be allowed back into Romania.

God worked extraordinarily as I went into Romania during the nine years prior to the revolution. I felt it was a miracle every time I crossed the border. Christian leaders were told by the dreaded Securitate (secret police) on several occasions that I would not be allowed to return. Yet, I did. It was amazing. Crossing the border of Romania became an exercise in prayer.

Many times, it was difficult to understand why border agents allowed me into Romania. Things had become very dangerous and difficult. In January, 1988, three friends from San Antonio, Texas travelled into Romania with my wife Tex and me. My wife and a couple from San Antonio left the country by train after a week of ministry. Brent Saathoff, who later became a board member of our ministry, remained with me for further ministry.

Just before Tex left Romania, someone broke into our vehicle and stole the papers for the rental car that we had picked up in Budapest, Hungary. We concluded it must have been the work of the Securitate because those papers were worthless to anyone else. We needed them to get out of the country at the end of the trip. So the question now was "What do we do?" Two Romanian friends living in Timisoara, Nelu Dronca and Pastor Peter Dugalescu, decided it would be best for me to report the stolen papers to the police so that I wouldn't have any problems when I tried to leave Romania.

I ended up spending the entire night at the police station. I was completely exhausted by the next day. After getting only forty-five minutes' sleep, I travelled to Arad and had lunch with another Romanian friend, Titi Bulzan. After lunch I told him I was completely worn out and needed a nap. When he later tried to arouse me to get ready to speak at the church, I got up and then collapsed. They lifted me back into the bed and let me rest a while longer, but when they came to see if I was able to go, I couldn't move. I couldn't even lift my head from the pillow. Titi stayed with me as everyone else went to the church.

Around eleven o'clock that night, I tried to get up and get dressed to go to a hotel. It was illegal to stay in someone's home. I told Titi I was going to try to leave. He helped me out of bed, and I went to the bathroom. As I looked into the toilet, the room seemed to be spinning. Titi sensed something was wrong and rushed into the bathroom as I was falling head first into the toilet. He saved my life.

Brent had been in another area ministering with Dr. Titus Coltea. They were shocked at my condition when they returned to Arad. However, Titi and his family nursed me back to health. Before we left Arad, I thanked Titi for saving my life. Brent, Titus, and I then travelled other areas of Romania. God blessed beyond anything I could have imagined. The final city where I ministered was in Alba Iulia. But the light that spread so rapidly caught the attention of the brokers of darkness. We were followed everywhere we went by the Securitate.

God moved in such a special way in Alba Iulia. People were so hungry for the word of God. It was amazing. The crowds came to everything we did. We had a youth service, but people of all ages showed up. Many people came to Christ, and we held "follow-up" sessions to teach the new believers how to follow Christ. However, it was not just the new believes who came to those meetings. The crowds were enormous. We had to move all the benches from the sanctuary of the church, and people stood packed against one another. The crowds flowed into the street. We estimated that more than 200 people came to Christ during the few days we spent in Alba Iulia.

Because of all that had happened, we were pretty nervous about leaving Romania. We didn't know what to expect as we headed to the border. It didn't take long to find out once we arrived. We were immediately pulled into a small office and questioned. Not long after the interrogation began, a plainclothes Securitate agent showed up and informed me that I would not be allowed back in the country.

I told the young woman who was interpreting to ask him why.

"You know why," he spat.

"No, I don't. What have I done?"

The interpreter was clearly terrified. Apparently, she wasn't used to anyone challenging a Securitate officer. "I can't tell him what you said. You'll be in trouble if you talk to him that way."

"Please go ahead and tell him. I want to know what I've done."

When she did, he was really hot. "You have broken our laws!"

"No, if I have committed a crime, you tell me what I've done. I've not done anything illegal." If I was going to get kicked out of the country, I wanted to hear it from his lips.

"One more minute and you're in serious trouble. Now get out of here."

We returned to the United States not knowing how serious his threat was. Brent made a trip back to Romania the following

June and didn't have any problems going into or coming out of the country. It gave me great hope that I would be able to return.

I decided to attempt to go back to Romania in August. Two friends, one American and the other a New Zealander, travelled with me. We met in Austria and took a train from Vienna to Oradea, the border city where Titus and Paul Negrut lived. About an hour before we arrived at the Romanian border, the three of us split up and went to different cars on the train. We wanted to make sure that if I had problems, the others wouldn't be associated with me and kept out of the country.

Normally, it took one hour for the passport check before allowing the train to continue into the country. This time it took two hours. I knew something was wrong. Finally, I knew what was wrong. Six soldiers came to the car where I sat. One of them said in English, "Mr. Tippit, please take your luggage and come with us." They took me off the train and soldiers surrounded me on the platform.

My heart palpitated. I saw my two friends looking out the window as the train pulled away from the station. As the train disappeared slowly into the distance, I felt as lonely as I ever had. Fear, fatigue, and the lack of information weighed heavily on my heart. No one told me anything— not why I was being blacklisted or why I was being kept under guard. One soldier was assigned to stay next to me while the others moved fifteen to twenty feet away. I stood. I walked in place. I sat on my luggage. And for a while I simply felt sorry for myself. I wondered if they would put me in prison.

About 3:00 a.m. I was chilled to the bone and depressed. Then the Lord visited me. He brought to mind the great old hymn, "Great is Thy Faithfulness," and I began singing. I then sang several of the great hymns that focused on the character of God—

"How Great Thou Art," and "Holy, Holy, Holy." Joy flooded my soul as I took my eyes off my circumstances and placed them on Jesus. I then realized something that caused me to chuckle. *I'm not their captive. They are my captives. They have to stay with me all night and can't leave.*

I knew a little Romanian and began sharing the gospel with them. Of course, the small amount of Romanian that I knew didn't last very long. By 5:30 a.m. everyone except me had fallen asleep. I noticed a small empty building. I was freezing. I decided that I could go in there and warm up. I would be able to see the soldiers if they woke up. As I entered the small building, I saw a bus pull up and people get on it. It was headed to Oradea. My mind was racing.

The passports of the people were checked when they got off the train, and it didn't appear that the bus driver was checking passports. I could grab my luggage and be on that train before the guards knew I was gone. For an instant, I seriously considered it. Was I up to it? I knew it would be foolhardy. I have to admit, though, there were moments when I considered making a run for the bus.

I didn't. They placed me on a train and deported me later that day. The last thing they said was, "Mr. Tippit, you will never be allowed back in this country. As long as you live, you will never again place your feet on Romanian soil."

I returned to the United States with a broken heart. I loved the Romanian people and had such dear friends. The thought of not being able to see them again ripped through my soul. Not long after I returned to the U.S., a note was smuggled out of Romania through acquaintances, telling me not to be discouraged. Titus told one of my colleagues who had made it safely into the country to tell me, "The glory of God comes through much suffering."

I kept those words close to my heart for a year. I prayed for Romania. Then the unthinkable happened. The Berlin Wall fell in November 1989. People asked me, "Will Romania be next?"

My response showed my lack of faith. "You don't understand. East Germany persecuted Christians, but it was nothing like Romania. That would be impossible. The Securitate is too strong."

One of the most extraordinary events of the last century took place the following month. An Evangelical pastor was to be arrested in Timisoara. Christians from numerous denominations gathered around his apartment to protect him. The Securitate came with soldiers and fired into the crowd, killing and wounding many. An emotional and spiritual explosion took place in the aftermath of the killings.

Thousands of people gathered in the main square of Timisoara in protest of the murders. Even though they had been taught from the time they entered school that God didn't exist, faith erupted in their hearts. Pastor Peter Dugalescu stood among the multitudes in the main square of Timisoara and preached. People shouted, "Există Dumnezeu! Există Dumnezeu! (There is a God! There is a God!) The people knelt with Pastor Peter and repeated "The Lord's Prayer."

This scene spread across the nation like a mighty tidal wave. The theme song became a song about the second coming of Christ. In one divine moment, the darkness was shattered. Titus sent an urgent message to me. "You must return to Romania immediately. The glory of God is filling the country."

I caught a flight to Vienna, Austria, and met a friend, Don Shelton. Even though my luggage didn't make it, I told Don, "We don't have time to wait. We must go immediately to Romania." We called Titus from Budapest and let him know when we would arrive at the border. We drove in the car across Hungary to the

Romanian border, the same border where they told me, "As long as you live, you will never again place your feet on Romanian soil." I knew my name was in the computer as an enemy of the state. We prayed the entire journey.

I'll never forget that night. It was cold. Snow was falling. We were the only people foolish enough to attempt to enter the country during a revolution. Everyone else was trying to leave. We pulled up to the passport control. Border guards rushed to our vehicle and told us to get out. I knew my name was in the computer as a person blacklisted from the country. I also knew the first question always asked was, "Do you have any Bibles?"

I took a deep breath as the border guards looked over our passports. Finally, one of them asked in English, "Are you Christians?"

My heart raced so fast I thought it would burst. I blew out a breath of air. "Yes. We're Christians."

I couldn't believe what happened next. The soldier threw his arms open wide and said, "Welcome to the new Romania!" Titus had been waiting for us and came running out of the customs building. We embraced. We shouted. We knelt and prayed. We gave glory to God— in the same place that they told me, "You will never again place your feet on Romanian soil."

Titus told me, "Everyone is waiting for you at the church. We must hurry."

I could hardly contain myself when we arrived at the church. Thousands of people had gathered. Everyone wept. We all rejoiced.

When I went on to the streets the next day, I witnessed things I never dreamed I would see. People ran up to us, shouting, "Există Dumnezeu! Există Dumnezeu! (There is a God! There is a God!) Everywhere Romanian flags flew, the communist hammer and sickle had been cut from its center. God spoke to my heart that the hole in the middle represented the vacuum in the hearts of the people.

We travelled to several cities throughout the nation. We visited our friends, Pastor Peter Dugalescu and Nelu Dronca, in Timisoara. We returned to Alba Iulia. People were so hungry to hear God's word. I'd never seen such hunger for God. Titus told me, "When the weather gets warmer, you must return and preach in the stadiums."

I did return in May to one city, Baia Mare. As we arrived, Titus asked me, "How does it feel to walk into history?"

"What do you mean?"

"This is the day that Pastor Liviu taught us to pray for. He taught us to pray that one day we would stand in the great stadiums of the nation and proclaim the gospel. God has answered our prayers today!"

I fell to my knees and wept.

I returned many times to Romania during the next few years and preached in stadiums throughout the country. I was overwhelmed with the grace and goodness of God when I preached in Alba Iulia. They had trained 200 counselors to minister to people who made commitments to Christ. One of the leaders told me, "Do you know who the counselors are?"

"No, I don't think so."

"They are the ones who came to Christ the last time you preached in our city before the revolution."

The following five years were incredible. The Romanians wanted to go to the former Soviet Union and preach in the stadiums there. Titus and I led a team of young people from Romania and conducted historic meetings in the stadium in the capital of Soviet Moldova. God worked mightily and the Moldovans said, "Let's go to Ukraine." We went to Ukraine and held historic meetings in stadiums throughout the Republic. Then we went to Siberia and on to cities throughout Russia that had never had an Evangelical church.

Perhaps, the most humbling place that I travelled after the revolution was a small town in southern Romania: Scornicesti. It was the birthplace of Nicolae Ceaușescu. Before the revolution, Christians were severely persecuted in that region. After the revolution, it became a despised place. Consequently, the town fell into deep poverty and despair. Some Romanian Christian youth decided to reach out to the town. The community had a poor water system, which produced many problems. The Christian youth from Oradea dug a well in the town and provided clean water for the people. They decided to start a church and have a special dedication of the facility.

They invited Dr. David Funderburk, the former U.S. Ambassador to Romania during the Reagan administration, and myself to speak at the dedication. I preached on Saturday and Sunday in the town square. Dr. Funderburk and I then spoke at the special dedication on Sunday morning. The dark dictator, Nicolae Ceaușescu, was gone. God's Spirit was present, and His glory manifested.

One of the reasons I've written this series is because of the hope that it brings to our hearts. I witnessed a nation enlightened by the glory of God. I know the potential dwelling in humble, praying believers. I've seen what God did in Romania and desire to see God's people in the West seek God for a mighty awakening.

I would be the first to admit that Romania has faced many difficulties following the revolution. It didn't mean that there weren't life issues they needed to face. God's visitation to the nation didn't exempt Romania from political problems. It didn't keep Christians from sin and make following Christ easy. It didn't provide a panacea for the economic ills or eradicate poverty. But it did change the nation. It dispelled the darkness. It brought freedom to people and gave them the faith to work through their circumstances.

The Romanians have given us a testimony of the glory of God. The Reformers left us a word several hundred years ago: *Post pennebras, lux! After darkness, light!* Before Mike Fechner passed, he uttered the one word that we desperately need today: *Awakening.*

My prayer is a simple one. "Oh, God, pour out Your Spirit today. Awaken Your people in this generation."

Above: Sammy Tippit, Dr. Titus Coltea, Don Shelton and border guards during the Romanian Revolution.

Below: Sammy Tippit preaching in stadium in Oradea, Romania after the Revolution. Dr. Titus Coltea translates for him.

This is the first paperback book in the series, *Light in the Darkness,* and is composed of three e-books: *The Approaching Darkness, Character in the Darkness, and God's Glory in the Darkness.* The second paperback book in the series, *Fire in Your Heart,* is scheduled for release July 2015. *The Suffering Giants* will be released August 2015 and *Praying for Your Family* in October 2015. The series will conclude with a full-length novel, which will be released November 2015.

For more information about the series visit: www. sammytippitbooks.com